YOUR TEENS AND SEX

Charles E. Wittschiebe

Review and Herald Publishing Association
Washington, D.C. 20012

This book was
Edited by Richard W. Coffen
Designed by Howard Bullard
Cover photo by Camerique

Printed in U.S.A.

Library of Congress Cataloging in Publication Data

Wittschiebe, Charles E.
Your teens and sex.

Bibliography: p.
1. Sex instruction—United States—Religious aspects—Seventh-day Adventist Church. 2. Sex instruction—United States. 3. Youth—United States—Sexual behavior. I. Title.
HQ35.W553 1983 649'.65 82-21396
ISBN 0-8280-0109-X

Dedication

This book is dedicated to the thousands of parents who
trusted me to share with their children
a deeper look into this gift of God
and
to their children, whose exuberance, curiosity, and acceptance
of me as an older friend
enriched both me and them.

A Strong Suggestion

When it comes to the subject of sex, young people today are thrown right into the middle of the pool. Newspapers, popular magazines, the entertainment arts, television, and conversations with their peers, all in one way or another touch on the subjects covered in my book *Teens and Love and Sex.* It is written especially for them.

However, I urge you to read that book for yourselves before you give it to your children. If you disagree with my frankness or my range of subjects or my treatment of the subject of masturbation, please refrain from buying it for them. (Most likely, of course, the book will come to their attention in some other way. My former book, *God Invented Sex,* for example, made the rounds many times in academy and college residence halls.)

I have asked the Lord to guide me in the writing. You will have to judge whether or not He has answered my prayer.

Contents

Preface

I thank the following persons for reading all or part of the manuscript for this book and that of *Teens and Love and Sex;* I appreciate their helpful criticism and encouragement: Dr. and Mrs. Edward Cross, Dr. and Mrs. Dale Nelson, Mr. and Mrs. Thomas Kuhlman, Dr. and Mrs. David Love, Dr. Charles Blomeley, Dr. Charles Anderson, Mr. and Mrs. Carol Edney, Dr. Judy Perry, Dr. Stanley Showalter, Dr. and Mrs. John Oliver, Dr. John Berecz, Dr. James Cox, and Mrs. Bobbie Strawbridge.

I thank Gloria Fincher Scruggs and Mary Lue Cochran for typing the original manuscript. Thanks are also due to Richard Coffen, book editor, for his generously shared professional competence and his supportive friendship. I am also deeply aware of the debt I owe to the copy editors and proofreaders and researchers, who do the indispensable bedrock work needed to produce a book.

Credit is due to the early Adventist pioneers in the field of sex education and to the men and women who are providing an increasing knowledge of sex within the framework of the Adventist faith.

Since the classes in sex education referred to in the books were composed of children from different denominations, it should be understood that I shared with them only information based on our common Christian heritage. The classes at the elementary school level were always divided by sex, and attendance was entirely voluntary. Because of the limits of time in the original classroom setting, *Teens and Love and Sex* covers topics in more depth than I normally presented.

I hope that these two books will strengthen the bonds between parents and children, providing for greater comfortableness in the touchy subject of sex education. To borrow a delightful phrase from one of my peers, I trust this book will assist you in becoming more "askable" parents.

Chapter One

Sharing With Parents

This book has been written primarily for Seventh-day Adventist parents in the United States. But since *God Invented Sex* received acceptance and approval from many people in other lands and cultures, possibly some of this material will also prove helpful outside the United States.

In this book I want to assist in the task of providing Christian sex education at home. After all, you parents bear the primary responsibility of educating your children in the basic elements of life. If the school your child attends already has a sex education program, this book should help you relate to it with greater effectiveness. Perhaps the book can open up another opportunity for communication between you and your child.

All of you have a stake in whatever type of sex education your children receive at school. The curriculum for Adventist church schools includes a section on sex education for seventh and eighth graders and for students in the eleventh and twelfth grades. However, few—if any—of our denominational schools offer a plan for sex education from the kindergarten to grade twelve. (At the time of writing, the Education Department of the General Conference was giving consideration to such a coordinated approach.) As concerned parents, you should press for more attention in this area of education. (Incidentally, the National Catholic Education Association has found "that the most popular programs in human sexuality are those which have corresponding courses for parents."

If your children attend a public school, you will want to know what type of sex education they are given. Remember that public schools cannot teach sex education in a religious setting. They must observe the strict separation between church and state. Some presentations of sex will range—on a Christian conservative scale—from amoral to immoral. Therefore, you have the extra responsibility to see that a balanced theology of sex fortifies the physiological and psychological facts that your children learn in public school. Obviously, the home and the church must supply this.

I have directed *Teens and Love and Sex,* the book for the young people, to both sexes. Welcome information about the opposite sex can be read by either with less embarrassment or self-consciousness. Since each may read the material in privacy, the more sensitive or self-conscious child (or one a bit immature for his or her age) will find the discussion easier to accept.

Before going any further, let me add right now that I would be fatuous and conceited if I thought that my book will provide all the necessary information for a young person or that it alone will evoke and encourage wholesome and balanced attitudes and feelings about sex.

In preparing the manuscript, I undoubtedly have made mistakes, both of omission and commission. I know a great deal more about the subject now than when my wife and I had to rear our children. Since those early years, 16,000 children have attended my sex education classes, in which I discussed the topic from our common Christian heritage. (I did not, for example, present our view of masturbation.) Many parents have shared their troubles and confusion with me. In the process of getting older, I have learned much. Please don't interpret this as an attempt at pontificating. Neither do I wish to create the idea that I have always handled things ideally and wisely. However, I do want to help other parents who walk the same road to share what I have learned and experienced.

Remember, doctors can have children who become ill; dentists, children whose teeth need much attention; law officers, children who get into trouble with the law; and ministers, children who do not provide the best example to other youth in the church. We all have to do the best we can where we are and with those entrusted to us. All of this, of course, with the guidance and support of the Lord.

The subject of the book is of first importance to the families of the church. In speaking of the family in our church, we usually picture a working father and an at-home mother who cares for their children.

Drs. C. C. Crider and R. C. Kistler, of Andrews University, have co-authored a trail-blazing book entitled *The Seventh-day Adventist Family: An Empirical Study.* (See bibliography.) They report that 59.5 percent of Adventist families have two to four children. They also state that a large number of Adventist wives work outside the home. We can safely assume that a large number of these working wives also have children at home.

Working mothers face additional problems, such as caring for children who are seriously ill (and possibly using up all their vacation time), or arranging for supervision during a teachers' strike. Practically all working wives carry an extra burden: having to do more than a fair share of the housework. One recent survey revealed that only 12 out of a hundred husbands of working women regularly carried a fair share of the housework. The divorced or widowed working mother has to carry all these responsibilities *alone.* Perhaps we ought to establish a hall of fame for our working wives!

It wouldn't be practical, though. Too many women deserve such recognition.

Another break with tradition influences many lives. The National Association of Elementary School Principals and the Institute for Development of Educational Activities, a division of the Charles F. Kettering Foundation, surveyed 18,000 children in 26 schools in 14 States. The study reports that one school child in five now lives with only one parent. In some schools, 90 percent of the children already live in homes like this. Estimates indicate that almost half of the children born in 1977 stand a good chance, sometime before their eighteenth birthday, of living in a one-parent family. Many youngsters, of course, live in one home and visit another. They are, in one sense, two-family children. In fact, Dr. Armand M. Nicholi II, a psychiatrist on the faculty of the Harvard Medical School, has pointed out that "one-parent families are growing about twenty times faster than two-parent families."—*Christianity Today,* May 25, 1979, p. 11.

Children from such families have school problems. As a group, these children earn poorer grades, are late to school more often, have a higher frequency of absences, and are more likely to leave school or be expelled than children from two-parent families. Separation and divorce cause emotional damage that shows up in the children's school careers.

Some of you have a child who has strayed from the path of Christian sexual behavior. You have wanted to maintain high Christian standards. At the same time you wanted to show your child unfailing love and compassion, so you helped him (or her) and his (or her) erring companion through an embarrassing and painful experience. Thus you have demonstrated the spirit of the father in the parable of the prodigal son. Please don't take this book as a condemnation. As brothers and sisters to each other and to our children, we must quickly close ranks around any hurt or misbehaving member and his or her immediate family.

As the servant of the Lord put it, "Parents may do everything in their power to give their children every privilege and instruction, in order that they may give their hearts to God; yet the children may refuse to walk in the light, and, by their evil course, cast unfavorable reflections upon their parents who love them, and whose hearts yearn after their salvation."—*The Youth's Instructor*, August 10, 1893.

This book rests on the basic premise that sex education inevitably occurs. The question is not whether, but what and when and how. Even a total neglect of the subject is a form of education. Parental silence conveys the message that sex is bad and that "nice" people avoid talking about it.

My main purpose in writing these books is to counter the trend expressed in such common statements as "too little, too late," "locking the barn door after the horse is stolen," and "throwing out the baby with the bathwater." I hope this book will keep unconcerned parents from becoming concerned grandparents.

Of course, no parent or grandparent is unaware of the pressures toward immorality in society. Even during middle and later years of life a distressing number of Christians fall prey to Satan's wiles. We need to remember Ellen White's startling statement: "The enemy will weave a spell of licentiousness around every soul that is not barricaded by the grace of Christ."—*Counsels to Parents, Teachers, and Students*, p. 257. This warning sounds strongly in my ears as I talk and counsel with our young people. My heart goes out to them. They live in a world notorious for its licentiousness. By the age of 16, one girl in five has engaged in sexual relations. Add three more years to the age, and two out of three have moved into this category. Before marriage, nine out of ten have engaged in sex.

Incidentally, I did not intend the occasional touches of humor in *Teens and Love and Sex* to develop any sense of levity or crudeness. I have used humor with the hope that it will serve as a lubricant and tension-reducer. This, in turn, will make it easier and more comfortable for our young people to absorb without threat a subject that has acquired a somewhat forbidding aspect.

Chapter Two

Sex and Your Teen-ager's World

Allurements from all sides challenge our young people to be sexy. Not wholesome or clever, or good or original, but sexy. The climate of the young people's world seems to have sex as one of its noticeable elements.

Daniel Lang, in investigating a flag-pledge conflict, had occasion to visit a high school in western New York. He wrote in *The New Yorker* magazine: "Student traffic was all around us, moving every which way to homerooms. The corridor seemed charged with sex. Wherever one looked, healthy, exuberant teen-agers were in frank flirtation; here and there they were in fleeting embrace." This school may be an exception, but the fact that this condition exists at all in any school should surely concern parents.

Dr. M. M. Kappelman, in *Sex and the American Teenager*, says that the teen-ager of today "accepts sex as a natural, biological, integral aspect of his everyday life." As a result, we now have a totally new subculture known as adolescent sexuality.

Society generally now regards chaperonage as a matter of the past. Automobiles allow much greater freedom of movement for today's teens, and for some it has become a relatively handy and movable bedroom.

In today's society sex has become detached from personhood. Individuals relate to it as a commodity in itself. Liberal voices urge sex for recreation, escape, and excitement. One recent book on sex in the college years, *Sexual Unfolding* by the Sarrels of Yale, has a section entitled "Recreational Sex." In the words of a *Time* article: "Self-denial is increasingly seen as foolishness rather than virtue."

Too many American youth no longer ask whether or not they should go to bed with someone. Instead they ask, with whom and under what conditions. (In fairness to the young women, I should point out that many of them who engage in premarital sex reserve this intimacy for men they plan to marry.)

Many modern young people reason that to be ready for sex in marriage, a person needs to obtain some experience before the wedding. They assume that familiarization with this aspect of married life before taking that step guarantees a better sex life—one that begins to be fulfilling much sooner.

The whole marriage structure strains under contemporary pressure. Many young adults ask such questions as How can one promise to love for life? What values does a piece of paper have in matters of the heart? Why not live together without marriage? Or why not choose "open marriage," which allows an occasional sexual relationship on the part of either spouse?

Sexual prowess has almost become the main criterion of normality. If a girl is a virgin, she worries that she may be frigid, neurotic, hung-up, or repressed. Many young people no longer respect virgins. They only assume that virgins suffer from a psychological aberration or an emotional illness.

A study of the loss of virginity among 35 university women reported that some women felt that their loss of virginity lifted a burden from them. The sexual experience made them feel more like women and adults. More and more women now consciously choose to lose their virginity. Practically every woman interviewed said she would be willing to live with someone on a trial marriage basis. These women, incidentally, are described as normal and highly valued students.

Many today experience a weakened guilt level over transgressions of the sexual code. "Engaging in sex is only human," they argue. If conducted discreetly, sexual misbehavior merits nothing more than a slap on the wrist, or more likely, for the man, a pat on the back.

The communication media are sources of stimulation. Advertising makes sexiness either an ingredient of many articles or an end result of using them. One can choose a sexy car or a sex-arousing mouthwash and toothpaste.

To add to the problem, girls enter puberty three years earlier than did their counterparts of earlier generations, and the age at menarche continues to decline. The grandmother of today's teen-agers began to menstruate at 15 and married at 18 or 19. She had no further obligation to go to school or to train for a vocation. Today's young woman may menstruate at 12 and not marry until she enters her 20s. Meanwhile, she usually has to spend more time in school to attain some proficiency in a vocation. Unlike her grandmother, she expects to work outside the home. As a result, she endures a lot longer period in which to control the pressures created by maturing sexuality.

Furthermore, educational institutions offer temptations and challenges. Eighty percent of coeducational campuses now offer joint housing for both sexes. The Sarrels of Yale state that young people in their junior year of college will find it very difficult to establish a sex relationship that does not include genital petting or intercourse. The Sarrels call today's American campus a "sexy place" and feel that college juniors find it difficult to keep themselves apart from this life style.—*Sexual Unfolding,* pp. 89, 64.

As further illustrations of the world in which our children are growing up, consider these items:

Television shows include homosexual roles. Some of the less fundamental religious communions and the moderate wings of some conservative groups are moving toward full acceptance of homosexuality as simply another form of sexual orientation. Many persons with such views endorse ministerial ordination of openly recognized homosexuals.

Concerned critics have voiced considerable opposition to the amount of violence on TV. But how much consideration is given to the erotic stimulation of our children? Many youngsters spend more hours in front of a TV set than they spend in school. Much of contemporary programming exposes them to portrayals of passionate lovemaking, sex-arousing clothing and gestures, as well as sadistic types of sexual encounters and the frank depiction of gay relationships.

A recent editorial in *The Charlotte Observer* (January 11, 1979) bore the title "Sex on TV—A Peep Show in Every Home." The editor commented: "TV already has nearly as much sex as a cheap motel that charges by the hour" and approaches sex "with all the maturity of a bunch of 11-year-old boys sniggering over pictures of naked women in a porno magazine."

Add to TV the impact of motion pictures and contemporary music. By their freshman year in high school, most students who attend the movies have seen X or R-rated features. In addition, the music they enjoy exposes them to suggestive tunes and lyrics.

No wonder that a leading authority in sex education says that today's teen-agers are "overstimulated, overfree, underprotected, and undereducated."

Ann Landers has stated that our sex-oriented culture is producing 13-year-olds "whose imaginations are seven years ahead of their emotional development." She concludes that modern young people cannot make "any distinction between love and sex."

One final point. Today's teen-agers have much more money to spend than young people of earlier generations. *Parade* magazine (December 11, 1979) reported that the average United States teen-ager has $22 a week to use as he likes and spends just about all of it. A Gallup poll found that those from 16 to 18 had $45 a week, whereas the 13- to 15-year-olds had $12 a week.

I think it is safe to guess that children of most Seventh-day Adventist parents most likely do not match the averages given in these reports. Nevertheless, they probably have a good deal more spending money, proportionately, than you parents had during your own teen years.

Chapter Three

Sexual Conditions and Prophecy

Morton Hunt, a popular researcher in the field of marriage and divorce, together with his wife, conducted a survey under the auspices of the Playboy Foundation. (This was a serious endeavor and had no overtones of sensationalism.) He reports on the results in a book published by Dell under title *Sexual Behavior in the 1970s.*

The findings are startling. Two out of three women and three out of four men don't feel that a woman who goes to bed with a man before marriage loses his respect. About half of all men and women do not regard homosexuality as wrong. Only one in four considers anal intercourse wrong. A high percentage of respondents favored premarital intercourse. And gonorrhea among teen-agers is the second most common infectious disease after the common cold.

Even more startling is Mr. Hunt's assessment of the speed of change in American sexual thinking and behavior. In his opinion, what has happened would normally take from 100 to several hundred years. From his evaluation of the present, he predicts that within five to ten years only a small number of men and women will remain virgins until marriage, and they will be the "deeply religious, the emotionally disturbed and the personally undesirable."—Page 150.

Perhaps Ellen G. White's statement that "great changes are soon to take place in our world, and the final movements will be rapid ones."—*Testimonies for the Church,* vol. 9, p. 11 can also apply to this aspect of society in the last days.

Other related predictions come to mind.

"We must not yield one inch to the customs and fashions of this degenerate age, but stand in moral independence, making no compromise with its corrupt and idolatrous practices."—*Ibid,* vol. 5, p. 78.

"Impurity is today widespread, even among the professed followers of Christ."—*Ibid.,* p. 218. "There is a strange abandonment of principle, the standard of morality is lowered, and the earth is fast becoming a Sodom."—*Gospel Workers,* pp. 125, 126.

"The uncontrolled indulgence and consequent disease and degradation that existed at Christ's first advent will again exist, with intensity of evil, before His second coming. Christ declares that the condition of the world will be as in the days before the Flood, and as in Sodom and Gomorrah. Upon the very verge of that fearful time we are now living."—*The Desire of Ages,* p. 122.

"Multitudes feel under no moral obligation to curb their sensual desire and they become the slaves of lust. Men are living for the pleasures of sense."—*Patriarchs and Prophets,* pp. 101, 102.

"I am filled with pain and anguish as I see parents conforming to the world and allowing their children to meet the worldly standard at such a time as this. . . . Parents do not know that secret vice is destroying and defacing the image of God in their children. The sins which characterized the Sodomites exist among them."—*Testimonies for the Church,* vol. 5, p. 78.

These quotations lead one to a staggering thought. If Ellen G. White penned them about an age that we today consider to have been Puritanical and Victorian, what would she say of today's conditions?

And should we not assume that the church in general will, along with its other departures from the scriptural teachings, also relate to the doctrine and practice of sexual purity with attitudes ranging from lukewarmness to sheer antagonism?

Living beyond the days spoken of—and far nearer the end than in Mrs. White's time—how can we fail to provide our youth with a theology of sex and a program of sex education based on that theology? We indoctrinate our children regarding the Sabbath, the Second Coming, dietary standards, and tithing. Should we leave out sex? We must recognize the very real danger that in its Laodicean condition the church may easily relate to the doctrine and practice of sexual purity with lukewarmness.

May I sound an encouraging note at this point? Wardell Pomeroy, one of the pioneer researchers in the field of sex and a highly respected sex educator, classifies as "mythical" the idea that today's young people are crazed sexually. *Who's Who Among American High School Students,* in a recent poll, found that 74 percent of the juniors and seniors they surveyed reported that they had abstained from sexual intercourse. Fifty-seven out of 100 planned to save this experience until marriage. This group, of course, comprises outstanding students—those most likely to be the leaders in their age ranges.

Chapter Four

A Christian Sex Education

Many parents make great sacrifices to furnish their children with an education in one of our Adventist schools. Yet do we equip them to meet the steady, insistent, all-pervasive pressures of the godless sexual world in which we live? If we wish to take a positive stand against laxity and corruption in morals, we must establish a code of sex based on a theology of sex. We also need to inaugurate a sex education program that deals sensitively with the biological and emotional aspects of sexuality.

This theology of sex will include the recognition that God designed men and women to be superb sexual creatures. The sex organs are marvels of bioengineering, not only in each sex itself but also in their remarkable capacity for fitting together—for one-fleshness. The anatomical provision of face-to-face intercourse sets human beings apart from the rest of the animal kingdom.

"The creator of man has arranged the living machinery of our bodies. Every function is wonderfully and wisely made. . . . From the first dawn of reason, the human mind should become intelligent in regard to the physical structure. . . . The children need to be instructed in regard to their own bodies. There are but a few youth who have any definite knowledge of the mysteries of human life."—*Child Guidance,* pp. 103, 104.

"It is the right of every daughter of Eve . . . to understand the mechanism of the human body and the principles of hygiene."—*The Adventist Home,* p. 87.

Note such statements as these: "They should understand the functions of the various organs."—*The Ministry of Healing,* p. 128. "Lead them to study that marvelous organism, the human system, and the laws by which it is governed."—*Ibid.,* p. 147. "Children are to be trained to understand that every organ of the body and every faculty of the mind is the gift of a good and wise God, and that each is to be used to His glory."—*Counsels to Parents, Teachers, and Students,* pp. 125, 126. "Every portion of the living organism is the Lord's. The knowledge of our own physical organism should teach us that every member is to do God's service, as an instrument of righteousness."—*Testimonies to Ministers,* p. 456.

None of these quotations specifically mentions the sexual organs, but obviously the phrases "the human system" and the "living organism" include them. The study of any part of the body—including the sexual part— will lead us to share David's enthusiastic awe: "I will praise thee; for I am fearfully and wonderfully made: marvelous are thy works; and that my soul knoweth right well" (Psalm 139:14). I particularly like the way the Jerusalem Bible translates this verse: "For all these mysteries I thank you: for the wonder of myself, for the wonder of your works. You know me through and through." Doesn't that expression "wonder of myself" especially warm your heart?

Much has been said and written through the years about the incredible complexity of the structure and functioning of organs in the human body. The brain, the eye, the ear, the heart, have all been praised and admired as marvels of creative power. Christians generally regard human beings as the climax of Creation week. We admire the human body as the ultimate in beauty, and we consider the human mind as the ultimate in earthly intelligence.

Since God created man in His image, no one has the right to call any part of the body dirty, beastly, or naughty. The sexual organs reveal God's wisdom and love and intelligence just as much as the brain or the heart or the stomach. The entire human body reflects His creative genius.

Think for a moment how easily and effectively the man's and woman's bodies can fit together. Each is designed for the purpose of uniting in one flesh. Not only is this true of the physical aspect, but it is equally true of the sexual emotions.

A woman's breasts not only serve a practical purpose in reproduction, but they also constitute a part of her attractiveness and one of her centers of sexual response.

The Creator placed in the sex organs of men and women sensory nerves capable of the highest intensity of feeling. All this in order to make intercourse an act with a special potential for delight and satisfaction. That's one reason why the word *climax* so adequately describes the culmination of *coitus*. This term can describe no other body function. We don't climax in eating or drinking or walking or swimming or even breathing.

The penis is designed to serve as an organ of elimination as well as an organ of lovemaking. (Incidentally, urine is not a dirty fluid. It is simply a germ-free waste byproduct from the process of living. The penis, then, does not become soiled by the passage of urine.) Although this is reasoning after the fact, it doesn't seem to me that God would have made an organ that has both a dirty function and one that should be extremely clean. The ability to shift the penis from its more usual function to that of intercourse lies in its astonishing structure. One psychiatrist, a specialist in the field of sexuality, has written that "a glance at the design of the caverns [within the penis] makes it evident that no human engineer could have invented these."

With words and diagrams, it takes a minimum of ten pages to describe the anatomical structure of the penis. To put it in a nutshell, the penis contains caverns that can fill with blood to make it firm and erect for intercourse. After intercourse, the blood flows back into the rest of the body, and the penis returns to its usual condition. This amazing double function of the penis makes the organ a marvelous creation in itself.

If, in our queasiness, we neglect to formulate a theology of sex and omit the study of sexual anatomy and physiology, of sexual intercourse, and of the good and bad in sex, how can we possibly encourage our children to read the Bible through once a year? In a cursory check of sexual references in my New English Bible, I find an average of one every 12 pages.

The children of the ancient theocracy of Israel had the commandments, laws, and statutes presented to them constantly. (See Deuteronomy 6:5-9; 11:18-21; 31:9-13.) The word *teach* in Deuteronomy 6:7 means "to whet," "to sharpen." One Jewish commentary indicates that the literal meaning here is to "prick them in." *The SDA Bible Commentary*, vol. 1, p. 991—in reference to Deuteronomy 11:19, a passage very much like Deuteronomy 6:5-9—states that the Jewish commentator, Rashi, interprets the words to mean "that a parent, from the time that a child *can speak* [italics mine] shall instruct him in the Hebrew language and in the Torah." On the related passage, Deuteronomy 31:11-19, the commentary states that "it is folly for children to be allowed to grow up in ignorance of the Word."

Obviously, then, children at that time heard both the

right and the wrong of the facts of life in the public reading of the laws. Furthermore, their parents explained these rules in more detail. Today, we are advised that "the principles set forth in Deuteronomy . . . are to be followed by God's people to the end of time."—*Prophets and Kings*, p. 570. Since Deuteronomy contains much sexual content, the inescapable conclusion is that all children of Bible-reading Adventist parents should ultimately understand the import of scriptures dealing with such material.*

*I asked Dr. Gerhard Hasel, a careful Old Testament scholar, if my inference from Deuteronomy was correct. He replied: "Regarding the questions on Deuteronomy 6:7; 11:19; 31:12, it is entirely correct that this material was read in the presence of the entire family, including children. Undoubtedly it was also explained to them. We must always keep in mind that in the ancient world people were much more open and much less restricted in talking about sexual matters. I am not sure how far back the Puritan silence regarding sexual matters can be traced, but it is certain that in Bible times people were much less complicated in their freedom to reveal matters relating to sexuality. In some sense it might be good for us if you could recapture something of that type of Biblical freedom without the license that in the mind of many people is a corollary."

Chapter Five

Two Parents and Sex Education

Very few children receive adequate sex education from one or both parents. Mothers generally deal with the subject of menstruation, but usually they do not discuss much beyond it.

With the onset of menstruation, girls have an obvious entrance into puberty. Boys have relatively little to compare to it. The signal of femininity sounds clearly in comparison with the spread-out indicators for masculinity in boys.

Most girls take pleasure and pride in reaching this milestone. Few boys have similar feelings about manhood when they experience their first nocturnal ejaculation. Menstruation is interpreted and prepared for, but wet dreams just happen.

Many parents resort to the avoidance technique in dealing with sexual subjects. Since men talk among themselves about sex much more openly than do women, I find it surprising that in many homes husbands regard sex education as the wife's job. One survey found that less than 5 percent of fathers ever open up the subject of premarital sex with their children.

One of the books that we believe inspiration produced is *Messages to Young People* by Ellen G. White. Can we introduce our young people to this book in a way that will leave them receptive and open to its God-given and well-meant advice? If they would accept Ellen G. White's counsel, they could avoid much grief during their premarital years and in marriage. Somehow our young people have come to view this book as preachy, repressive, old-fashioned, unrealistic, and unsympathetic to their longings and desires.

A second look at Mrs. White—the warm, human love she had for her husband and he for her, and their happy and satisfying marriage—would help make her messages on premarital behavior more welcome.

Messages to Young People can serve as an introduction to the material in *The Adventist Home* and *Child Guidance* that is pertinent to the needs of young adults. An intensive and realistic study of marriage and parenthood provides one of the best motivating forces for intelligent and self-controlled conduct during the premarital years.

Reading, of course, only serves to introduce a young person to the wide-ranging subject of sex. Christian sex education, obviously, must grow out of sound training in Christian character and living. Worship—not just formal, but vital, adapted to the children's level of development—is an integral part of the process. Do you make worship a part of your family's religious experience, a daily reminder of the priesthood of the father and the supreme role of motherhood in the plan of God?

The whole tone of the home should play its part in training children to be as nearly ideal lovers and spouses as possible in this less-than-ideal world. We can give our children no greater gift. Homes that produce fine husbands and wives are priceless in their value to the church and to the state. They are a boon to the next generation coming on the scene. The father-mother-child relationship is the matrix for all later receiving and giving of love. The addition of siblings broadens the developmental field and contributes strongly to later love capabilities.

Not only do our young people have a right to knowledge about their sex organs and sex psychology, but they also have the right to know about the various methods of contraception by which they can later regulate the size of their families. When our young people live up to all the standards of the Christian life in the realm of sex, knowledge about contraception will not lead to any misconduct. Dedicated young Christians will make the proper use of it when the right time comes. Meanwhile, it is reassuring for them in these days of the high cost of living and the need for small families to know that they can have a happy and fulfilling marriage without the risk of being burdened with more children than they can properly care for. Most mature Seventh-day Adventists know of Mrs. White's comments on this matter.

The Pill—as one method of contraception—is so widely known and referred to that it would be a rare teen-ager who does not know what the term alludes to. Many boys know about condoms. To a lesser degree, young people know something about foam, diaphragms, vasectomies, et cetera.

If your daughter, to your dismay and despair, has chosen to live by the loose standards of the day, then she definitely needs all the information she can get on protecting herself against unwanted and unplanned pregnancies. It is sad if she chooses that way of life, but it is sadder still if she enters it without the knowledge that could protect her from the painful choices of marrying because of pregnancy, becoming a single parent, adopting a baby out, or arranging for an abortion.

A report by Zelnik and Kantner reveals the disturbing statistic that only 41 percent of single 15- to 19-year-old young women know when in their menstrual cycle they are more likely to become pregnant. Thus they can't even have the protection that comes from knowing the "safe period"—even though that hardly guarantees avoiding conception.

We should not regard having a baby as the well-deserved and fitting punishment for misconduct. The baby and other innocent bystanders are likely to suffer unhappy consequences—*some of them lifelong.* One of these, for example, is the effect such an episode has on younger brothers and sisters and the damage this does to the sanctity of the moral standards advocated in the home.

An unwanted pregnancy that goes to term brings another human being into the world. This innocent baby must share whatever consequences arise out of the particular circumstances of his or her conception and birth. Who has the right to do this to another person?

Some of us, then, despite our best efforts, may have a child who fails to live up to the sexual code we and our church profess and teach. Such behavior can be a symptom of emotions that are not primarily sexual in nature. Often the misbehavior is a form of rebellion against you or the church. It may be a young person's way of "getting even" for real or fancied unfairness in discipline. Sometimes it may be a reaction to a too rigid posture in sex, coupled with an absence of sex education or with a type of education that is essentially negative and debasing.

If you suspect that your child suffers from such an emotional condition, try to get him or her to a counselor who can gain the child's confidence. The young person must not perceive this individual as an undercover agent for you. A professional counselor can probably draw out the youngster's anger, and work toward rebuilding a more compatible relationship between you and the disturbing (and disturbed) child. You, of course, will respect the confidential nature of the counseling role and will not try to pump the counselor for information. The therapist can, however, share anything with you that your child permits him to.

As one man has put it, the finest start in sex education that a father can give his children is to love their mother. Parents can do a bit of "smooching"in the presence of their children. You don't need to conceal love pats, kisses, and hugs from your youngsters. Open displays of affection make the child realize that their parents care for each other and that they like to touch each other. The young person also benefits from the parents' unself-consciousness in expressing their feelings. The child senses that home base is secure. (I do not mean to encourage vulgarity or suggestive remarks.)

One of the most poignant questions asked by a young person during a series of meetings on Christian sex and marriage was, "What can you do to convince parents of 45 years—married 25—that it's not too late to be 'lovey-dovey' and romantic when they have been unhappy for years?"

The father's role is important in all phases of sex education. He can reinforce—by contrast and by interaction—the mother's model of femininity and thus nurture the development of his daughter's awareness of femaleness. As he brings out and enhances his wife's femininity, this in turn has an indirect influence on how his daughter sees herself as a woman. She unconsciously picks up many clues as to what constitutes male and female behavior and how a man and woman can live together happily. As she matures into womanhood, she will feel more adequate in establishing relationships with fellows. In a general sense, when a woman knows one man well, she knows something about all men.

You would logically expect fathers to show a particular interest in the sex education of their sons. Yet they often evade this responsibility. The situation is rather odd, since men traditionally have acted as though sex was a subject for the strong, unshockable male rather than for the delicate, sensitive woman.

Actually, in one sense, women see more of "sex" than men. Mothers regularly bathe boy babies much more often than fathers bathe their daughters. Baby-sitters are almost always girls, and so they must take Johnny into the bathroom and help him keep his pants dry while he urinates. When out shopping with her little son, the mother can take him into the ladies' room without any embarrassment. If a father were to take his daughter into the men's room, he would probably cause one or two heart attacks among the men. One cartoon shows a mother shedding tears as her little son goes into the room marked GENTLEMEN.

Yet, in spite of all this, mothers are often amazingly ignorant of their own sex biology and psychology—not to mention that of their husbands. However, mothers are important teachers of sex. A survey by *Seventeen* (July, 1970) reported that mothers provide most sex education for girls. This is probably so because menstruation is a definite point of development that mother and daughter can't avoid. In addition, the young lady has much more at stake if she has an unwanted pregnancy.

However, more than three fourths of the girls polled felt that their mothers should not have had to handle sexual subjects by themselves. Mothers often will explain reproduction and the basic mechanics of intercourse, but they often either omit or deal slightly with the female sex drive and orgasm, with contaception, and with sexually transmitted diseases (venereal diseases). The young women quite generally felt that a qualified school teacher is the best single source of sex education. Incidentally, in listing the single most important item they thought a course in sex education should cover, the physiology of reproduction ranked first, and methods of birth control came in second.

Here are a few suggestions for the mother-teacher.

If you encourage your daughter to talk freely with you, be ready to hear things that may upset you or disturb you. In fact, you may find yourself in definite disagreement with some of the opinions your child will express.

Talking about sex usually is a more emotionally charged experience than most other exchanges. If you don't have a warm and trusting relationship with the ability to share ideas or feelings woman-to-woman, frank talks on sex most likely will never occur.

A knowledge of your own feelings and attitudes is imperative. Unless you have positive, warm, and comfortable feelings about sex, negative currents will flow between you and your daughter that will block the free flow of ideas or will cause them to come through in a distorted form. You need to be aware lest any unfortunate experience in your past sexual life will color your whole attitude toward the subject. It can make you avoid certain areas either from fear of self-disclosure or to avoid the pain or fear of shame they evoke.

Keep in mind that your daughter is moving into womanhood with its sense of independence, and yet at times she remains your little girl with a great need of you. Sometimes she will treat you as though you were retarded or hopelessly "out of it." At other times she will seem angry with you for no apparent reason. Expect these things as a part of the ups and downs of the adolescent phase of development. They don't mark you as a failing parent.

Gordon Shipman tells of a mother who related to her daughter's first menstrual period in a highly unusual way. After showing her daughter what to do for the flow of blood, she took her to the living room, where her father was sitting. She told him: "Well, our little girl is a young lady now!" Her dad hugged her and congratulated her. She felt grown-up and proud that she was really a lady at last. The child rated it as one of the happiest and most exciting days of her life.

I related this experience to a young mother, and she took a different view. "I'm not sure how that approach would have affected me [the hug and congratulations],"she mused. "I remember how mortified I was when Mamma announced she was going right downstairs to tell Daddy. I begged her not to. I had even tried to pretend it wasn't there until I woke up in the morning with blood all over me and couldn't hide it."

Parents will try to be sensitive to their children's emotional natures. They will tailor their approach to their children's varying personalities.

Chapter Six

The Single Parent

It is difficult to give a definite figure for the number of single Adventist parents. The General Conference Home and Family Services do not, at this time, have any statistics on single parents within the church. PHILOSDA, in its bulletin for November, 1981, states that the church is full of people without spouses, and children with only one parent. Estimates indicate that the Adventist Church in the United States serves from 160,000 to 200,000 unmarried, divorced, or widowed members.

Joseph Bayly, in *Eternity* of February, 1982, discusses the problem of the single person in the evangelical Christian community. He reports that between 1970 and 1980 the number of divorced men in the United States increased by 150.9 percent, the number of divorced women by 118.8 percent, and the number of never-married women by 89.2 percent.

He summarizes by estimating that in 1980 almost 7 million more people were living alone than in 1970. PHILOSDA put it another way by estimating that at any one time 12 percent of Americans will be living alone.

Most single parents have become so by divorce. Almost 90 percent of these individuals will marry again (but of such remarriages, almost half will lead to a second divorce, with its share of heartache).

Divorce, of course, never completely severs the relationship. This is physically and emotionally evident when there are children, even when one parent has almost entire custody. Until a man's former wife remarries, her "existence" intrudes itself into the life of the second wife. The first wife may use the children as a pretext for making many telephone calls to her former husband, asking for advice or assistance, reporting disciplinary problems and illnesses, mentioning the financial pressures, et cetera. The second wife feels tied to the former wife by an invisible cord and suffers much emotional stress. A former husband tends to be less intrusive. But often only the remarriage of both parties will reduce the capacity for disturbance.

Remarriage, of course, opens up many potential occasions for friction and strain. Here are some. A divorced woman with children and sole custody marries a divorced man with no children. A divorced woman with children and sole custody marries a divorced man with children and sole custody (not so common). A divorced woman marries a divorced man with children but not custody. And vice versa. A widow with no children marries a widower with children. A widow marries a divorced man with children but not custody. A widow marries a divorced man with children and joint custody. A widower marries a divorced woman with children and sole custody. And so on, with other types of custody. To make the situations a bit more complex, let us assume that one or more children are born in the second marriage. In any case, about 70 percent of all divorces involve children.

Spouses in second marriages have to make all the marital adjustments necessary in their new relationship and all the parental adjustments involved in a relationship that is not "natural." It has to begin as purely "legal," but then, one hopes, it will go on to freely chosen emotional ties.

Children usually suffer most in divorce. Either they are glad to see the break come, despite the emotional scarring it causes, or they would like to have the marriage continued, which leaves them with a different type of emotional damage. The second group can feel a lot of anger over the tearing apart of their life patterns. Most divorced and remarried persons with children report that the children do as well or better in the second marriage. However, a survey reported by Judith S. Wallerston,* based on a five-year follow-up on such children, found that a little more than 60 percent of such children ranged from happy and thriving to reasonably well.

Obviously, it is difficult to be "single" after being married. (Widows and widowers don't feel the same kind of singleness that divorcees do. In fact, sometimes widow(er)s and divorcees do not feel entirely comfortable with each other when in small groups.) Getting back into the dating pattern is a major step. And children can complicate the dating arrangements in terms of hours, propriety, and trying to balance parental responsibilities with the strong wish to find and marry someone who will be the kind of mate hoped for in the first marriage. Your children, depending on their ages, may be jealous of your dates. A teen-age daughter may go on another track and try to outshine you in physical attraction. Children can so eagerly desire a replacement of the missing parent that they urge you to marry the first likely prospect on too short acquaintance. Living alone with children has its particular liabilities: the practically total responsibility for discipline and guidance; the balancing of parental care with working hours; the special crises

*Quoted in Gerald and Myrna Silva, *Weekend Fathers* (Los Angeles: Stratford Press, 1981), p. 63.

presented by illnesses and accidents to parent or child; the loss of trusted and well-liked baby sitters; the pressure created by particular crises, for example, a teachers' strike; the attempt to meet the children's emotional needs by oneself; the lack of escort to social functions; the fear of robbery and rape; the maintenance or severing of relationships with the previous spouse's family (grandparents, aunts, and uncles); the lack of places where single friendships can comfortably be initiated; the need to adjust to the feeling of being a fifth wheel in small "couple" groups.

Age, health, years of marriage before divorce, relations with the spouse's family, type of custody, nearness to original homes, vocational abilities—these factors may compound the problem. If you are a couple moving toward divorce I recommend that you read Gerald and Myrna Silva's *Weekend Fathers.* Acting on their advice could mean a more equitable arrangement in divorce, or, better yet, might even lead to a deeper reconsideration of all that is involved. You may decide to seek help in reshaping your marriage so that it will meet the vows that you made at its beginning.

Basically, one's commitment to the Lord, in terms of maturity and sincerity, is for the single Seventh-day Adventist parent the central support in all periods of life.

When you begin to date and the possibility of greater intimacy with a particular person seems to be building rapidly, you should intend to stay within the bounds of what is proper and moral in your conduct. It surely is not news to you, if you are a woman, that men—divorced or single—seem to think that a widowed or divorced woman is coping with a strong need for physical sex—a need these men are more than willing to meet. Some women too seem to be reaching equality with the men in this area and freely engage in casual sexual contacts.

Since you have been married, you are an experienced

person in sex. If you have been disappointed by too much or too little, or with mates whose ideas were "kinky," you will be on your guard against a repetition of such experiences. Honest frankness with your new friend should help protect you, and you do not need to engage in premarital sex as a way of checking each other out.

An important article appeared in *Christianity Today,* May 25, 1979. H. I. Smith, a specialist in single-adult ministries, wrote on "Sex and Singleness the Second Time Around." His findings are based on the singles of a large church in California. These persons identified themselves as born-again Christians. (He cautions that generalizations about behavior and attitudes cannot be made from this one small group. However, the report can certainly make any church member wonder how alike or how different the situation is in his or her own church.) Here are some of his findings.

"One fourth of the men and almost one half of the women found celibacy unrealistic." In keeping with this attitude, only 9 percent of the men and 27 percent of the women had remained celibate. The most disturbing item, in my estimation, is the statement of one woman who did practice celibacy. She said that she had "to hide this fact *even* from church people." Women in her situation who say No are viewed with amazement, or as if they had something wrong with them. Usually they are not approached again for a date.

I think we have to admit, regretfully, that abstinence from sexual relations during separations or a period of divorce may not be the sexual code of some Adventists, as well. And probably we can all agree that this interval of singleness can be the stiffest test of one's commitment to the principles of a Christian sex life.

Surely we would all agree that your conduct ought to be in keeping with the moral guidance you have given your children (or plan to give them). Morton Hunt, in *The World of the Formerly Married,* states that nearly all formerly married persons "have one set of morals for themselves and another set for their children."

If you are a divorcée and your former husband became involved in an affair accented with sex, you may think that your husband's strong sex drive and his poor control of it played a large part in the breakup of your marriage. You may therefore unconsciously carry some resentment against sex. ("What else do they ever think about?") This naturally makes healthy communication with your children less likely. In fact, you may avoid dealing with the subject altogether, because of the feeling it evokes. If, in spite of your divorce, you still have a healthy and cheerful feeling about sex you surely have the basis for a sound sex-education approach to your children.

If the father is the only parent present in the home he can accept responsibility for introducing his daughter to the subject of menstruation. If he feels reluctant to do so, then he should arrange for some woman to act as his surrogate. Or he can inquire whether the school his daughter attends will offer an acceptable presentation on menstrual hygiene for the girls.

Basically, the father should provide the best model of manliness for his son. Of course, this will include the father's capacity to express affection freely with his child. Mrs. White writes that "the reason why there are so many hardhearted men and women in the world is that true affection has been regarded as weakness, and has been discouraged and repressed."—*The Desire of Ages*, p. 516. The healthier the relationship between father and son, the less likelihood there is that the son will show sexual deviation later.

Today's boys must grow up in a changing world in which their fathers and mothers are reacting to the challenges of the women's-liberation movement. Newer definitions of masculinity and femininity are emerging.

Most boys have more female authority figures as role models than they have male role models. The great majority of teachers in the elementary grades are women. It is probably not just a coincidence that the more masculine boys often receive lower grades. I have been pleased to see the increasing number of men who teach in the elementary grades, men who don't consider their nurturing profession a threat to their image as virile men. At the same time, we must not forget the millions of women who have generously and wisely shared with the American home the responsibility of bringing countless boys to competent and decent maturity.

One of the saddest statistics in American society is that one child in ten lives in a fatherless home. Yet having a father present physically in the home does not always make a great difference. Professor Urie Bronfenbrenner, of Cornell University, has referred to a study of middle-class fathers with 1-year-old infants. The fathers studied spent only an average of twenty minutes a day with their children. But data collected by microphones attached to the babies' shirts revealed that the father averaged only thirty-six seconds daily of intimate interaction with the infant.

Bill Moyers recently interviewed children in their early school years. He asked: "If you had to give up, forever, either talking to your father or watching television, which would you choose?" A majority preferred watching television instead of talking with their dads.

As has been mentioned, some fathers spend very little time with their children. However, the quantity of time is less important than the quality. Sometimes parents and children can be in the same room for hours, yet very little communication takes place. One of my counselees, a young woman of 23, said her father often would read a newspaper during her attempts to talk with him.

What gives this tremendous seriousness is the fact that the basic gender identity—male or female—can be permanently formed in the short time of approximately the first two and one half or three years.

Stressing the father's role, as I have just done, only intensifies the loneliness and concern of the single mother with a growing son or sons. Some of you mothers have been widowed, divorced, or separated. You are trying to bring up your boys all by yourselves. You lack a male role model in the home.

Your son's association with other males should be as natural as possible and in line with the level of personal and sexual development to be expected during that particular time in the boy's life. Sudden and abruptly arranged doses of "man" can have a jarring effect.

Single mothers will need to guard against being too protective of or too emotionally close to their children. This single-parent role places extra demands on you. It forces you to be more conscious of the male role and the need to supply the proper nurturing atmosphere for it. The presence of a husband and father usually takes care of this automatically. You may even unconsciously place your adolescent son in a kind of substitute-husband role, to his detriment and that of the other children in the family. (In *God Invented Sex* I stated that the church has a responsibility to give more assistance to single parents. See pages 254-256.)

Much more could be written on this subject, but the limitations of space prohibit. One television ad recently evaluated the responsibility of the single woman parent in a roughly humorous way. It said that the two hardest jobs for women are being a single parent and being an undercover cop.

Permit me to add a personal note. Over many years I have had great admiration and respect for the way many single parents—particularly women—have bravely and gallantly gone through the pain of divorce and devoted themselves unselfishly to all the needs of their children. I imagine that a special section in heaven's book of remembrance is reserved for such parents.

Chapter Seven

Sex and the Climate of the Home

A climate of love and trust puts certain boundaries on the parents' right to invade the privacy of the late teen-age child. Surely parents should respect their youngsters' letters and diaries as confidential documents and not open them without permission.

"Satan and his host are making most powerful efforts to sway the minds of the children, and they must be treated with candor, Christian tenderness, and love. This will give you a strong influence over them, and they will feel that they can repose unlimited confidence in you. Throw around your children the charms of home and of your society. If you do this, they will not have so much desire for the society of young associates."—*Testimonies*, vol. 1, pp. 387, 388.

Notice two significant points in this quotation. One: Treat them "with candor," which means frankly, openly, and sincerely. Two: Your candor will help them feel that they "can repose unlimited confidence in you."

Sexual matters need to be handled comfortably but not as though you were dealing with spelling or woodworking. The topic is loaded with emotional and spiritual elements that you can share with your children. At the same time, avoid grimness. Humor and a light touch will help when you discuss those points that might produce tension and self-consciousness. Avoid presenting sex as a not-and-don't subject, largely negative and mainly composed of warnings against all the possible evils and dire consequences.

Keep your communication at the child's level. As he grows he can return to the same subject later and tune in on a higher level. Remember, however, that children know more than most of us realize and are more sensitive than many of us recognize.

When two parents are comfortable with the topic of sex and find sexual fulfillment in their marriage, their attempts at sex education will most likely come across to the child with a positive effect. Such a young person can more readily accept his parents as models for his own sex life.

Despite their best efforts, some parents encounter the heartbreaking experience of seeing a child go astray. These parents need to remember that the home is not the only world of the child. Negative and sinful forces are always at work. Sometimes these hindrances are quite obvious, and at other times they infiltrate deeply before parents even become aware of their existence.

After all, some parents with rare advantages have had straying children—Adam, Noah, Isaac, Manoah, Samuel. Even the father in the parable of the prodigal son, who represents God, encounters a discouraging relationship with his two sons. Today many a denominational leader has endured sad experiences with his children. These individuals did the best they knew or were aware of at the time the children were growing, and they still deserve our respect and loyalty. (How, too, do we explain the "good" children of "bad" parents?)

When He judges your children, Jesus will take into account the circumstances that have shaped their lives. (See *The Desire of Ages*, p. 568.) In fact, He shows a special concern for those who give trouble. He looks upon these children with pity. "He traces from cause to effect."—*Ibid.*, p. 517.

Doubtless your central function as parents is to be loving authority figures for your children. In this sense you represent God to them. The love you evoke engenders obedience and respect. It leads to an increasingly voluntary incorporation of your wishes and commands in the form of self-control and self-government. More and more your children will take over their own self-direction.

In the process of bringing up children, American parents are more likely to err on the side of permissiveness than on the side of strictness. However, it is far better to have a firm code of behavior with occasional reasonable exceptions than to have a loose one with occasional fitful periods of firmness. No matter how rapidly your children may develop biologically and sexually during their teen years, they still lack the emotional maturity and spiritual stability to control and direct their sex drives.

As an example of permissiveness, *Time*, as long ago as 1962, reported the doings of some preteens. Girls under 12 wanted nylons and garter belts, had regular beauty shop appointments, and wore training bras. Boys and girls of this same age attended dinner dances, the boys in tuxedos and the girls with corsages. Both sexes engaged in "making out" with variations of post-office and spin-the-bottle. Some mothers encouraged their fifth- and sixth-graders to date. In fairness, it should be noted that this report covered the behavior of children in the "better" suburbs. (You will note that the clothing and game details of this report are already dated. But do you think the situation has improved during the past 20 years?)

Young girls are often pushed too early into overstimulation. They are dressed like animated Barbie dolls and encouraged to act on a level of sophistication beyond their years. Instead of developing as persons, they begin too soon to measure their worth and standing in terms of their "success" with boys. Many a parent with an attractive young son knows how often he is pestered by phone calls and transparent approaches from such girls. These girls become sexy without being feminine and do not realize that a truly feminine woman is per se sexy (in terms of being attractive and attracting to males). As one woman writer recently put it, "Perhaps in a few years little girls will become extinct altogether."

Parents who permit or encourage conduct of this sort reveal their own immaturity or irresponsibility. The goal—popularity at any price—makes popularity of questionable quality, and the price paid far too high.

Strictness, however, must "have a heart." Children learn to fear but not to love parents who display a "dignified, cold, unsympathetic" air of authority. "Some of the most valuable qualities of mind and heart are chilled to death."—*Fundamentals of Christian Education,* p. 68. You are urged to smile and unbend from your dignity, to adapt yourselves to the children's needs, and to "make them love you. You must win their affection, if you would impress religious truth upon their heart."—*Ibid.*

This doesn't mean that parents should be pals to their children. Their pals accept them for what they are and expect them to reciprocate. You, however, are responsible for their education and discipline during their formative years. As they mature into adulthood the love between parent and child can be enriched with the affection of friend with friend.

If you are like most parents, you are trying to do your best to rear decent children. Although you should be able to see your own mistakes, don't magnify them out of all proportion. You cannot take all responsibility for the direction of your child's life. It is not easy to see how many unusual advantages have helped "good" parents and how many negative influences have victimized "bad" parents in their efforts to rear their children.

Parents have the right to set limits for children's curfew and dating. These boundaries should be reasonable and in harmony with the practice of the best homes in the community. In fact, it is not a bad idea for parents to get together and set up rules and regulations for the children of the area. This would prevent a child from jockeying one parent against another. It also would protect parents from being compared with others to their disadvantage. A too-lenient home in the neighborhood can create problems for those parents who want to be strict but in a fair and understanding way.

Chapter Eight

Our Denominational Past and Sex Education

Despite the importance of sex education, Adventists have done very little concerted planning to direct our children in their sexual development. And this is in spite of a Joint Council of the Educational and Missionary Volunteer departments of the North American Division, held in St. Helena, from June 4 to 14, 1915. Notice the date! Since the council minutes are practically "museum pieces," I feel that you will be interested to read what was said so long ago. It sounds pertinent for us today.

At the meeting C. C. Lewis in his address stated that "parents almost universally shirk this duty. They are not prepared to discharge it, or are afraid of it, or entertain a false modesty in regard to it, and hence have entered into a sort of unconscious 'conspiracy of silence' upon the subject. . . .

"Now all this ought to be remedied. This subject is a proper one for parents and children to talk about. . . .

"To overlook these opportunities, and go on year after year without alluding to these subjects, is in my judgment either false modesty or unwarranted neglect."

To meet the need, he proposed that the Missionary Volunteer Department prepare and circulate "purity literature" and that the Department of Education, through the Fireside Correspondence School (now the Home Study Institute), offer a brief course to prepare parents and teachers for giving instruction on purity subjects.

Elder Meade MacGuire opened the discussion that followed the address. "I feel that this is one of the most important subjects that we have to deal with here in this Council, because, next to religion, this is the most important question in the world, the question of sex, the relation of men and women. Yet it is one which we seem willing to ignore, or let alone, perhaps because of the difficulty there is in discussing it. . . .

"In the first place, it seems difficult for adults to appreciate the real conditions under which a child grows up in this day. The conditions have changed greatly in the last thirty or forty years, since some of us were boys and girls. The conditions have changed very much in the last five years. [1910-1915]. The children today are subjected to temptations that those of us who have reached maturity can hardly imagine. . . .

"Now it seems to me that in some way or other we ought to educate the teachers and young people's workers so that they will wake up and make a special study of this subject, and be able to help these young people and childrei Shall we know a question of such importance, and one which affects many more of our young people I am satisfied, than the majority of us have any idea of, and ignore it, or do nothing for fear of making it worse? or shall we do something?"

It is pleasing to note that a woman took part in the discussion. Matilda Erickson commented: "Judge Lindsey says that nine tenths of the social impurity comes from ignorance. . . .

"I heard a social purity lecturer say that one of the chief contributing causes of the downfall of our boys and girls today is the songs they sing. . . . I find that light reading is considered one of the chief causes of impurity. . . . As to amusements, one of the leaders in the purity federation says that moving picture shows and theaters are not safe places for young people, because they drag so many down. . . .

"I lay great stress upon the dress question. . . . In a leaflet on social purity it was stated that unless there is a radical change among our young people on the dress question, there is little hope of making progress in social purity and the social purity cause."

Twenty-nine years earlier, Dr. J. H. Kellogg spoke on social purity to an audience in Battle Creek (*Social Purity*, an address delivered at Battle Creek, November 28, 1886, by J. H. Kellogg, M.D., Battle Creek Health Publishing Company). He said, "Personal impurity is sapping the vital energies, debasing the mental faculties and blunting the conscience of thousands of youth. . . .

"The time for silence, for timidity, for false modesty, for prudishness, has long passed.

"Many of the papers and magazines sold at our newsstands, and eagerly sought after by young men and boys, are better suited for the parlors of a house of ill repute than for the eyes of pure-minded youth. . . .

"The almost universal habit among boys and young men of relating filthy stories, indulging in foul jokes, making indecent allusions, and subjecting passers-by to lewd criticism, is a most abominable sin. . . .

"Womanly modesty is a quality which is becoming, in many social circles, quite too rare. . . . A certain forwardness of manner is becoming exceedingly prevalent among girls as well as boys. . . .

"Excessive familiarity of the young of both sexes in social intercourse, tends in a most decided manner to break down the barriers against impurity, and to prepare the way for the most flagrant violations of purity and chastity."

And nine years before that, June 28, 1877, to be exact, Elder James White wrote an article for the *Review and Herald.* He entitled it, "Safe-guards for Students." He talked about discipline and restraint and rules in our school, and then quoted extensively from an article in *The New England Journal of Education* captioned, "The Outlook for Womanhood." The content is worth quoting, even if the language is a bit quaint.

"In many of our communities, there is getting to be no small occasion for concern with reference to the future womanhood of our girls. They are thrown at the very outset into the very rabble of the mixed school. Little restraint is thrown about them in their association with the boys. Little proper girlhood guidance and instruction is given them. The text-book and the recitation are everything. The manners and the modesty of the girls are nothing. If she has been delicately guarded at home, she becomes half-hoiden [sic]. If nature or home-neglect has made her hoiden [sic], she becomes brazen.

"In society and the home, foolish talk, and loose-gossip or scandal; precocious petty novel-reading, and newspaper sensationalism with that crowning evil, unreasonable and insane child-parties, quicken into premature life the passion for beau-seeking, until the minikin miss and the manikin master must have their confidential notes and arm-in-arm promenades, à la Abelard and Heloise in disgusting miniature.

"Arrived at her greenest teens, the promiscuous intermingling of the evening party, and the corrupting familiarity of the kissing-bee; the undisguised pairing-off of the popular lecture and the evening service; the dancing-club, the evening promenade, and the night ride, make the false child-fancy a headstrong passion, that is alike regardless of parental restraint and womanly self-respect.

"As the result of all this premature association, and

false sex-training, we see the girl, in her own practical estimation, *nothing* as a true, pure, self-sustained, home-blessing woman; but filled out complete, and for the first and only time, *something*, when she has a fellow at her side; and, as a natural consequence, without much regard to anything touching his education, character, position, and prospects; practically everything being summed in his one sole virtue of being simply a male human animal.

"In our smaller communities, this is becoming so painfully common, that the modest, self-controlled young woman, at once the pride of the home, the pure influence in society, and the domestic foundation and hope for the future, is the exception, not the rule. And so we are fast swinging loose from the old Saxon anchorage of true domestic virtue, and drifting broadside into the over-mastering currents of mere Parisian frivolity and sex-dissipation.

"In the midst of the over-growing laxity of manners, the multiplied stimulants to precocious passions, and the increasing facilities afforded by devilish art for the indulgence of illicit gratification, we cannot safely trust it to take care of itself. Observant fathers and sensible mothers are becoming painfully conscious of the growing evil, and alarmed for the prospective purity and happiness of their children, and the coming households."

Another quotation, from the *New York Tribune* reprinted in the *Review and Herald* of May 17, 1870, offers a sad commentary on that period: "The parental character has been growing weak and inefficient. Not only is there too much reliance upon our system of public education, but there has been a pretty general abdication of parental authority. Children do not love or at least do not treat their parents with the ancient piety. They are disobedient without repentance and disrespectful without remorse. Kindness awakens no gratitude, and self-sacrifice no sense of obligation."

And, finally, in the later years of the last century, Ellen G. White conveyed the distressing information that "there is not one girl in a hundred who is pure-minded, and there is not one boy in a hundred whose morals are untainted. . . . The curse of this corrupt age is the absence of true virtue and modesty."—*Testimonies,* vol. 4, p. 96.

You may ask why I have quoted so freely from "the good old days." First, I wish to make it quite obvious that in many ways they were *not* the "good old days." Evidently, Adventist parents have never lived during a time of marked purity and high standards of social behavior in which to rear their families. Second, I want to ask: Do conditions in our world today make it easier for us to guide our children in their sex development as young Christians?

Certainly prophecy does not indicate a gradual improvement in mankind's condition as we near the end. The signs we see around us corroborate the prophecies of Paul and Peter and the extensive implications from the Spirit of Prophecy for these days.

I think one of our leaders, in a highly responsible position, summed it up well: "We are living in a period when both the world and the church are giving more attention to proper sex education. A few decades ago we probably, wrongly, as a church and in our educational systems, made only very scanty reference to the sex program and gave almost no education and counsel to young people on this subject."

The long quotations about conditions in the past began, you remember, with recommendations made at an important council nearly 70 years ago. Do you wonder why we have not responded to the wise advice offered at that time? And when you consider how much worse conditions are today and how little preparation for this aspect of life we have designed for our children, do you feel chagrined, ashamed, guilty, surprised, and afraid?

These feelings are heightened by the realization that sex education can be given only in the safest way in our own educational system. In our church schools the educators base their teaching on a profound reverence for God as Creator, Sustainer, and Sanctifier. They look to His Word as the foundation for all instruction in sexual behavior for the Christian.

If today we continue to fail to deal with the subject of sex adequately, our young people have the right to conclude that the subject is not important. Or they may decide that it is not a proper subject for discussion and therefore deduce that sexual knowledge is basically dirty and has no place in Christian education.

The forces of evil, of course, don't share this reticence. They make the subject a central concern in all aspects of communication: speech, music, literature, moving pictures, TV programs, photography, and word of mouth. By their boldness they practically claim a monopoly, and the Christian, by default, seems to concede that claim. Whenever we do not work positively against these evil forces that operate against our children, we are, in effect, abetting them. Having provided no armor for our children, we leave them vulnerable to attack.

Chapter Nine

Parents as Sexual Persons

As a basis for all effective sex education, parents must comfortably and happily accept the sexuality of their children and all that it implies. In fact, right from the beginning of life the sexual nature is marked off and emphasized. Unless a woman has been deeply concerned about the physical condition of her baby, her first question will be, "Doctor, is it a boy or a girl?"

Parents communicate their feelings about sex as potently by their attitudes and the sex-emotional climate of the home as by a conversation. In referring to instances of sexual misconduct, adults may pass them off in a jesting manner, or describe them with heavy-handed vulgar humor, or imply a certain amount of grudging admiration and envy toward the persons involved. Children have a built-in radar by which they pick up these subliminal messages. And when the signals received on their radar don't agree with the words that they hear, they will grow confused and lose trust in the spoken word.

Parents need to ask themselves: Are we embarrassed to have our teen-agers see us as sexual persons? Would we rather have our children consider us to be above such behavior—hormoneless, passionless, almost neutered persons? Will this provide an escape from the blush-producing self-consciousness that sex discussions with teen-agers often seem to arouse? Children can reinforce this tendency by their own difficulty in accepting adult sexuality. Our understanding of their feelings and ideas can surprise them. They tend to forget that all fathers and mothers were once children and adolescents—that they have wondered about the same things, suffered the same anxieties and fears, and endured varying degrees of loneliness as they matured sexually.

College students do not seem to imagine their parents being active sex partners. A survey of 646 Illinois State University students whose parents were still married revealed some interesting opinions. Practically all the students considered their parents as happily married and "still in love." But more than half of them thought their parents had intercourse "once a month or less." The researcher summarized the findings: "Apparently most of the 90 percent of students who felt their parents were happily married and still in love believed they maintained this happy state without the help of sex, or at least not much of it."

A teacher of human sexual behavior reports that when he asks his students if they can imagine their parents having intercourse, only one in four can. And only one in 13 can imagine his grandparents being sexually active.

This is probably one reason why children don't always open up to their parents about boy-girl relations from petting to intercourse. They seem to feel that they would really shake us up and make heavy waves between us and them. (They may also assume that such a discussion would show them up as not being as well-behaved and dependable as we think them to be.)

The unresolved sexual conflicts of parents may also hamper straight-forward communication with their children. Some of you may not have lived too pure a life in your earlier years and now feel hypocritical if you expect more from your children. As two parents put it in a note to me, "Your talk was of much help to us, as it brought a problem to the surface. One which we must now face and try to deal with. Our daughter J—— was expected before we were married. We feel that maybe she should know this, but we don't know how to tell her. More than anything else we want our children to grow in these Christian concepts. Can you help us?" Of course, this type of embarrassment faces parents as soon as the child can recognize the difference between the date of marriage and his birthday and the normal nine-month period for pregnancy.

If you find yourself in such a situation, you can frankly tell your children that your past misconduct occurred because you were not Christians or because of a lapse in your dedication to Christian principles. Christ has forgiven and cleansed you, and now you want your children to have the happiness and peace of mind that comes from obeying the Lord's counsel in sexual matters. You want the strength of your present commitment to Him to help them.

You may have been reared in such a negative way regarding sex that you still find it hard not to think of sex as something too basically wrong to be enjoyed even with your husband (or wife). In such a case, you will require almost a "conversion" to understand that sex is clean and a God-given source of great pleasure.

Naturally, it would be surprising to learn that your children have never interfered with your sex life. Pregnancy alone causes a break in the rhythm of intercourse. The new baby often seems to be on the new mother's mind more than her husband's needs for sexual intimacy. (Women seem to be able to operate on two circuits in this area.) Through the years your children have no doubt occasionally deprived you of the privacy you needed for spontaneous lovemaking. Their needs often had priority. Sometimes their presence nearby made you wonder whether you could be heard while you engaged in intercourse and thus prevented you from freely expressing your feelings. (The matter of bedroom privacy is discussed elsewhere in this book.)

In any case, many parents do not find it easy to talk about sex. Some still think it is not a "nice" subject. Today's freer attitudes and seemingly universal preoccupation with sex serve only to make them more aware of their reluctance to discuss sexuality frankly.

Lack of knowledge about some of the biological and psychological aspects of sex may increase some parents' diffidence in approaching the subject. Despite contemporary freedom and greater knowledge about sex, many parents (especially mothers) are surprisingly ignorant when it comes to sexuality. Every now and then, when I have shared with parents the range of depth of sex knowledge I planned to cover with their children, mothers have suggested (sometimes humorously and sometimes seriously) that they could make use of such a class for themselves.

On the other hand, guard against too early sophistications. Girls, for example, should be girls before becoming women. They should enjoy the whole period of natural unselfconsciousness before moving into adulthood. The awareness of their sexuality should not dominate all their relationships with boys or men. Parents should discourage a precocious interest in cosmetics and hairstyling, in fashions, and in so-called sophisticated behavior.

Permit me to mention an incident. A group of parents asked me to conduct a sex education class for their children. The program was entirely voluntary and would be for both boys and girls. One mother asked permission to sit in with the girls. She had been married 16 years, and she had not had a natural child. Her two adopted daughters—both in their early teens—enrolled in the class. I didn't want the mother present since it might put a damper on her girls' willingness to ask questions. However, I left it to the girls whether or not Mother should stay, and they graciously granted permission. During the class, I made it a point to watch her out of the corner of my eye. She listened intently and, without speaking, evidently appreciated the spirit and content of our discussions. About a year later I saw her sitting in the front seat of her car. She held a new baby in her lap. I walked over and said to her in an incredulous tone of voice, "Yours?"

Looking at me with a smile of mixed happiness and embarrassment, she said emphatically, "Yes! My husband says it's because of that class!"

Incidentally, embarrassment in discussing the subject of sex is not confined to mothers. Quite a few fathers avoid such discussions and leave this area for their wives to take care of. Even the most sophisticated people sometimes avoid dealing frankly with the subject. David Niven tells of a world-known friend, with 27 godchildren, who sidestepped a frank question about the copulation of two dogs. The child asked, "Look at those two little doggies. What are they doing?"

"The little doggie in front," the godfather said, "has just gone blind, and his friend is pushing him all the way to St. Dustans."

With sex education provided today in many schools and with the great amount of information available in newspapers and magazines and on television, the average parent has to make an effort to keep a few steps ahead of his child. Note that we are talking here only about information. Parents do have the great advantage of experience. Don't let your child's purely factual information and his occasional know-it-all attitude make you forget the big edge you have. Even when a child has engaged in sex a few times, he cannot match your longer, deeper, and more mature experience.

Sometimes parents become jealous when their children go to "strangers" for information about sex or to get help with a sexual problem. If the person involved is morally sound and has a healthy interest in your child's welfare and happiness, you can be glad for the extra help. No parents can meet all their children's emotional needs. The parents may be away when the situation arises, or the child may fear that his negative attitudes will get him "in wrong." In the latter case he seeks a more neutral person. When the emotional distress results from tensions between the parents and the child, then it is almost too hard for the child to turn to his parents for help. How, for example, does a child get helpful and healthy sex education from a parent who thinks that sex is dirty, who considers it an unwelcome chore, bribe, or weapon, or who feels too embarrassed to speak about "such things."

At all times parents should remain aware of the danger of projecting into their children's questions or behavior their own sexual experience. A man of 50 and a young man of 15 can both look at a girl in a bikini, but the fantasies of each may vary because of the great difference in maturity and experience. It is hardly fair to impute to a young person fantasies and ideas possible only to a person with years of living and then to punish him for the guilt aroused by this act of projection.

Comfort yourselves, however, with the knowledge that even the experts are not perfect. A leading sex educator who has said and written some beautiful and helpful things about sex, several years ago related a conversation that took place in her own family. Her 17-year-old daughter said to her one day, speaking about her younger sister of 14, "Mother, you've done a very poor job with Marie. She has no idea of what a boy suffers when she behaves a certain way."

And this leading educator agreed with her daughter's judgment. "You never do as well with your own as with other people's children, and I'm no exception," she confessed. She added that many girls from 14 to 16 are unaware that a "boy responds instantly with an erection to almost anything—perfume, actions, words—and miniskirts." Speaking for parents in general, she admits that girls have not been told what they can do to avoid embarrassment and potential danger.

Chapter Ten

Sex Education: Staying Abreast

Fundamental to all the attempts at educating children in sex matters is the realization that adolescence is the most challenging, provocative, annoying, delightful, scary, encouraging, and trying period for both parents and children. One authority says that *change* is the name of adolescence. Another says that the best adjective to describe this period is *ambivalence.* These two descriptive terms should prepare us to accept the peculiar stress of helping a child through adolescence. No wonder someone has commented that the most difficult role in life is to be the parent of an adolescent.

Adolescents want and need to depend on you, yet they are eager to try their own wings. They respect your judgment, but they also want to assert their own "wisdom." They love and hate. They want to be understood, yet they often pull into themselves. These puzzling mood swings are unpredictable.

Psychologist John Rosemond recently wrote about the "terrible tweens!" his catchy name for 11- and 12-year-olds. He stated that this age period can be miserable for the tweens and their parents. He called the "tween-ager" a "rebel-in-search-of-a-cause" and an "emotional basketcase," careening wildly from one extreme to another. Tweens are unreasonable, painfully self-centered, unable to decide whether they want to be dependent or independent. And the same usually holds true for teens as well.

Parents who share sex knowledge and feelings find themselves caught up in these push-and-pull forces and usually suffer some setbacks and failures. The whole experience of relating to an adolescent is often much like riding a roller coaster or taking a trip down a river with rapids and whirlpools. But to continue this last analogy, there is beautiful scenery along the way—the trip is exciting—not time for boredom—and relative peace comes upon the arrival at the destination of adulthood. If we keep praying, loving them, and rolling with the punches, we most often will see them come through this period without disgracing us or suffering permanent damage themselves.

At the same time, remember that no two children ever find themselves in the same family (we are not speaking of multiple births here). The first child comes to inexperienced parents, who probably intend to bring him up as a model child and not like the many brats they have seen. The second child is welcomed by more experienced parents and also must learn to live with a sibling who has the advantage of seniority. The third—well, you can finish the rest in your imagination. We also have to consider the changing circumstances in which children are born—the family's home and neighborhood, the level of income, the closeness of the parents' original homes, the kind of schools available, the health of the parents, and so on. In this sense, no two children are ever born to the same parents or into the same family. And each child requires an approach based on his or her own emotional receptivity and readiness.

In addition, all children are different. One child may be quite open about his curiosity, another will be too shy and reticent to discuss personal matters, and the third lies somewhere in between. One child will have a strong interest in his sexual organs and seems to be heading for a long period of intense masturbation and sexual involvement; another may seem so little interested that he appears to be pointed toward a life of celibacy. One worries us because he has too much interest in sex, and the other because he seems to have too little. Furthermore, a child growing up with brothers and sisters is much more likely to pick up the basic facts of life, at least in terms of anatomy, than a single child.

In any case, the younger the child the more primitive and biological his sexual behavior. As he moves up to adolescence, he develops emotionally and socially and acquires attitudes and ideas that color his sexuality and make it in one sense more psychological and, Christian parents hope, more spiritual. Crossing the puberty line allows entrance into the heterosexual world with all its accompanying effects on the still-developing sexuality. However, through these years the growing understanding of his being created in the image of God should exert an elevating and supporting force in the control and direction of the sexual nature.

A safe, general rule is to stay abreast of your child. Help him absorb ideas and feelings at his own rate of speed. Also learn as much as you need so you can answer ordinary questions on reproduction, sexual practices, and sick, or evil forms of sex. Your own experience and reading will provide you with information on foreplay, intercourse, orgasm, and other details of intimate lovemaking. All this is to rest on a theology of sex obtained from your careful reading of the Scriptures and the writings of the Spirit of Prophecy.

Children's level of tolerance for sex information will differ from family to family and from child to child, depending on the internal emotional climate of the home and the openness of communication between parents and children. At one family camp in the South, I met a 15-year-old girl who was reading my book, *God Invented Sex,* in order to evaluate it for her parents. This was certainly a surprising switch from the usual order of "censorship," and it may be the only one of its kind! On a Caribbean island I spoke to an American missionary mother about the book, and she said she was encouraging her 14-year-old to read it. On the other hand, some parents would have a heart attack if they saw the book in the hands of any child below the age of 18.

Some parents evade the responsibility of sex education by stating that the child has not asked any questions about the subject. Yet parents do not usually wait for their children to initiate comments and instruction on matters such as finance, recreation, music, dress, choice of companions, and social habits. Practically every area of life is addressed without waiting for the child to bring up the subject. Why, then, is this critical area of life chosen as the one in which the child arranges the timing of communication? Isn't this waiting for the child to ask questions simply a rationalization for our self-conscious and embarrassed unwillingness to take the initiative?

Parents must approach their children with the truth before the children's peers (and other sources) provide erroneous information and before exposure to adult levels (films, magazines, personal contacts) opens them to corrupting influences.

It is much better for the child to know the truth from the beginning rather than having to unlearn error before hearing truth. Nature abhors a vacuum. The devil is tempted to fill up all empty spaces, especially those in the brain of the Christian.

A protracted period of indifference to sex on the part of your children is not necessarily something to congratulate yourself over. Such a lack of interest could arise from inhibitions caused by anxiety triggered by misinformation, hidden fears, or unwarranted guilt.

Sometimes your children will not ask questions about sex because they hate to admit that they don't know everything already. They may want to appear as someone who knows "where it's at." Such cases need extra tact.

You, in turn, may not know the answers to some questions. Simply tell your children that you had not thought of that one but you will look up the answer and share it as soon as you find it. A reasonable number of "I don't know" answers will not shake young people's faith in your adult wisdom.

Perhaps I should state here that in communities which provide well-planned programs of sex education in their schools, parents frequently find themselves quite ignorant regarding some areas brought up by the children. And then there may be rare occasions when your children's quick perception or startling insight almost overwhelm you.

A number of years ago, *Life* magazine ran a series on the beginnings of life. One of the pictures portrayed an ovum with the millions of sperm cells swimming around. The daughter of one of my psychiatrist friends was questioning her mother about which sperm would be responsible for the baby. The mother replied, "The one that gets there first."

The little girl became very thoughtful for a moment, then broke into a beautiful smile as she announced with great pleasure: "You mean we're all winners!"

Usually, your children's peer group will exert more influence than the home or the church on their behavior. For this reason, the peer group is one of the main sources of information on sex. Children are naturally influenced by their associates. They want their friendship and their esteem. And they want to belong.

To the degree that the home and the church and the

school omit sex education from their programs, to that degree will the influence of other children increase. They will gladly teach "the babies" all they know, including their large fund of misinformation and experience in questionable practices.

Sometimes our frankness at home and our comfortableness with the subject of sex can lead to some embarrassment in public. One girl of 5, traveling in a streetcar with her mother, asked, "Mother, when will Daddy put another seed in you so that a baby can grow?"

As you educate your children in the proper names of sex organs and their functions in sexual intercourse, advise them not to share this information with the neighbor children. Tell them that these frank chats are for the family and are a special kind of intimacy that we reserve for those we love. Inform them that not everybody thinks cleanly and comfortably about sex and that some have attitudes and practices contrary to the high standards we support.

Chapter Eleven

Privacy and Nudity in the Home

In a recent meeting one participant asked, "What do you do when your preschool children walk in on you while you're making love?" And from another meeting: "When I was young I used to hear my parents making love, and I thought my dad was hurting my mom. Can this cause real hangups in my sex life? If so, how does one get rid of them?"

By way of specific answers to these questions, the father can tell the child that he and mother were playing together, sort of wrestling around and making love at the same time—that the sounds he heard were not sounds of pain but sounds of pleasure. (After all, wrestling matches between friends can be fun. The accompanying grunts and groans don't indicate pain or anger or fear.)

Some children who see their parents engaging in intercourse suffer deep anxiety. They may conclude from what they see and hear—as did the second questioner—that Daddy was hurting Mommy. At the same time, they may recognize somewhat hazily that the confusing act also involves a peculiar intimacy different from ordinary fighting.

One intensive study of women's sexual feelings revealed that those who as children had seen or heard their parents engaging in intercourse always spoke of this with deeply negative feelings: shock, revulsion, and even indignation.

Dr. William A. Block tells the story of a 9-year-old girl who suddenly became mute and remained so for three months. Treatment by the family doctor, the pediatrician, and hospitalization for two weeks made no change in her condition. Finally, a child psychiatrist penetrated to the cause of the muteness. The night before the onset of her muteness, the child awoke feeling sick and went to her parents' bedroom. She saw them apparently wrestling roughly and heard sounds she thought came from pain. Feeling that she had accidentally found out that her parents were doing something bad, she unconsciously froze into a mute condition. The revelation of the secret to the psychiatrist and his comforting explanation as to what really had happened, opened her lips. Appropriately, her first words to him were, "Thank you."—*What Your Child Really Wants to Know About Sex and Why,* pp. 114, 115.

This case is unusual. A marked failure in sex education and a poor emotional climate in sex doubtless underlay the girls hysterical neurotic reaction. After all, probably more than half of this world's children have frequently been exposed to their parents' engaging in intercourse. For many persons, separate bedrooms have not been a way of life. (I wonder, sometimes, how much privacy there was in Jesus' home.) "Natural" sex education and constant familiarity with the facts of life in their normal setting prevent harmful emotional effects on children in such cultural conditions.

Dr. James E. Simmons, coordinator of Child Psychiatry Services at the Indiana University School of Medicine, said that his work in a public clinic had brought him many patients whose housing arrangements made it highly probable that the children had seen their parents in intercourse. Yet in dealing with the children who suffered from a variety of emotional disturbances, he had not come across one case in which such exposure had much to do with their emotional distress. He felt that the parents in such cases usually suffered the most, not the children.

Some parents, because of discomfort or embarrassment, refrain from ever discussing intercourse with their children and sometimes give the child the impression that the subject is either dirty or shocking or both. If a child then catches his parents in the act of intercourse, he may lose respect for them because he finds them engaging in something he considers bad. He regards his parents as being two-faced.

Additionally, even though he has stumbled on the situation innocently, he feels like an interloper or trespasser and therefore likely to be punished. Sensitive parents will give him an opportunity to put his feelings into words and then deal with these emotions in a comfortable manner.

If either parent seriously worries about the effect of such an encounter, the chances are that he or she should take a good look at his or her basic feelings about sex. Professional help might be in order for the parent and not for the child.

Brothers and sisters should generally have separate rooms as early as possible in their lives. Sometimes it is not possible, of course, and usually there are no unwelcome effects. But occasionally the sharing of the same room can set the stage for premature overstimulation, leading to unhealthy sex games or solicitation of sexual favors by an older child (example: a preteen boy with his younger sister).

Likewise it is not unreasonable or unloving if parents place a child in his own room by the time he enters his second year. Sharing a parental bedroom sometimes leads to sexual overstimulation accompanied by anxiety and guilt. On the other hand, a young child may want to share the bed of a parent of the opposite sex because of feelings of anxiety or to gratify a sexual impulse. Usually, however, these children develop normally into adults who can function healthily in their sexual relations.

More likely it is the parents' sex life that suffers in these situations. The child's presence puts a damper on sexual activity. The parents try to maintain quietness so the child won't awaken. Sex activity can't begin until the youngster has fallen asleep. Having always to be alert to the chance of the child's waking up cuts down on the spontaneity and freedom that should characterize love-making.

When traveling, some families ease up on the rule of privacy at night. To save on expenses all will sometimes sleep in the same motel or hotel room. Most families can take an infrequent vacation like this in stride without any damage to the normal custom at home. Under these circumstances, probably most parents postpone any engagement in sex until the children have fallen sound asleep or until the family reaches its destination.

If a father has a work schedule that makes the afternoon a more appropriate time for intercourse, the children should be trained not to intrude on the parents' privacy at certain hours of the day or when the bedroom door is closed (and locked). The youngest child does not need to know what the parents are doing, and the parents need not feel embarrassed if the older children do guess.

One youngster, by way of example, sensed (at her age level) the meaning of the locked door. An operating room team was talking about children's interest in what their parents do and about their propensity for walking in at odd moments. One nurse reported that just before Christmas she had locked herself in her bedroom so she would not be interrupted while she wrapped Christmas presents. Her 8-year-old daughter tried the door, and in an excited tone said to her older sister, "Mommy's locked the bedroom door, and Daddy isn't even home."

It is reasonable to conclude, then, that as children get older they can understand why the door is sometimes locked. Parents have the right to keep the bedroom door locked or to insist that no one enter without knocking and waiting for permission to come in.

Margaret Mead has pointed out that in the United States, parents feel they should keep their children from getting neurotic misconceptions of sex by often being nude in the presence of their children. Such behavior does not, however, seem to protect children from becoming confused or fearful and from rejecting sex.

Parents who shower with children of the same sex can establish another channel of sex education. On the other hand, some data have indicated that continuing exposure to parental nudity can psychologically damage the child. Of course, one should be aware that the disparity in the size between parent and child can make a deep impression on the child, especially in the case of father and son—when the latter is at eye-level with his father's genitals. A mother's breasts may almost overawe her daughter and make her wish that she could grow up more quickly.

Probably most Seventh-day Adventists would agree that nudity between parents and children of the opposite sex should be confined to accidental, unavoidable exposures. When exposure occurs, parents should handle the situation gently and with humor and avoid accusing the child of being a peeping Tom. Reasonable attention to privacy will avoid most embarrassing encounters.

If a girl walks into an unlocked bathroom and sees her father naked, the sight of his genital organs may cause her to react with distress, fright, or revulsion. Such a situation can be handled much more comfortably if sex education has begun early and in a manner commensurate with the child's development. Once again, a touch of humor can alleviate much of the embarrassment. The word *oops*, for example, can relieve the strain, especially if it is toned just right. A touch of comedy often averts tragedy.

Children develop sexual feelings early in life and can early have sexual fantasies. Seeing parents often in the nude or having habitual body contact in such a condition can cause a kind of sexual arousal that children find difficult to handle. Some children may react by pushing aggressively for continuing intimacy of this kind, by masturbation, or by withdrawal into themselves.

Society takes it for granted that people will wear clothing, and by the time children are a few years old they have made this assumption part of their way of life. So little sister says to little brother, "Stay out of here. I'm dressing," and pretty soon he is saying the same thing.

Becoming "reserved" in speech usually takes a bit longer. Sometimes children will, without inhibition or self-consciousness, bring up subjects that adults find very embarrassing.

For example, a cartoon I saw some years ago showed a church wedding scene. The bride and groom were standing in front of the minister, and he had just finished pronouncing them man and wife. A little boy loudly asked his mother, "Does he put the pollen on her now?"

Dr. Lendon Smith tells of a mother who was grocery shopping with her 6-year-old daughter. When the mother placed a box of sanitary napkins in the cart, the girl asked loudly, "What's that?"

"It's a box of sanitary napkins," answered the mother, embarrassingly aware of the other customers within hearing distance.

"What are they for?" continued the daughter.

The mother's hands tightened on the handle of the cart as she replied, "Grown-up women use them."

The daughter then abruptly asked, "Where are the cookies?"

Parents need to deal with personal privacy, nudity, and sex talk in a way commensurate with the age of the children. As a youngster grows older, the parents may be more insistent on maintaining their own personal privacy but more open in discussing sexual topics with the child. And when the child moves into adolescence, parents will want to increasingly respect their teenager's privacy.

Chapter Twelve

Sex Education: Basic Elements

Before you attempt educating your children in matters of sex, you need to clarify for yourself how you feel about sex. If you regard it as dirty or hush-hush, you will convey this to your children. And in their minds what is dirty when they are 6 or 9 or 11 continues to be dirty when they are adolescents and adults. Unhealthful sex education casts a long shadow over the life ahead. Unless of course, someone with wholesome and cheerful ideas of sex removes the negative impression you have imposed on your children.

Approach the topic of sex not with fear but with reverence; not with threats but with protective information; not with God's frown on it but with His smile. In practical ways you can describe it in the broader context of the aims of Creation and redemption.

Present sex to your boys and girls as a function they will both engage in some day for happiness communication, intimacy, and oneness. Don't condition them to view it simply as an aggressive act performed on a surrendering woman.

Past generations stressed the procreation element in sex—how else could one carry on the family name or provide grandchildren for one's parents? How else could the couple prove themselves to be normal?

Today this goal in sex receives less emphasis in premarital and marital planning. Thus we should focus even more attention on the elements of happiness, communication, intimacy, and oneness. In short, sex education today is not mainly an explanation of the reproductive process. Nor should we understand it primarily as insurance against premarital sex, pregnancy, or venereal disease—as a way of keeping children out of trouble. In the words of Dr. Steven Homel, who devised the sex education curriculum for the department of education in Pennsylvania: "The cause of pregnancy and venereal disease is not sexual relationships. Needs in emotional and social spheres and the interactions and emotions are the basic causes."

Always keep in mind that children who have not entered puberty cannot (because of immaturity) understand the meaning or experience the feelings involved in mature sex. Children can be taught to engage in sexual activities (for example, in pornographic films), but they are very much like talking parrots. The bird's words sound human, and Polly seems to know what she is saying, but all this has to be rated in terms of the bird's brain. Any circus can show animals doing "human" things, but only the ignorant would impute to the animals a human awareness of the meaning behind these acts.

Sex education is not just a presentation of biological facts. These serve, of course, as the nuts and bolts of the machine, but the facts alone do not explain why the machine was made or how to provide the power and control to make it function effectively.

Sex education is not a process of punishing or shaming a child. One of the most pathetic illustrations of such an approach came to me in a letter. "I am curious also as to what you *personally* would do if you found your 14-year-old son in possession of magazines showing women in sexy, naked positions? Would you castigate him in front of his two college-age sisters and their future parents-in-law? Would you drag him down to the local newsstand, all the time shouting how the newsstand is polluting him? Would you make statements to the effect that he was on the very verge of patronizing whores because of viewing these magazines? As a matter of fact, all these things happened to me."

"Love, the basis of creation and of redemption, is the basis of true education."—*Education*, p. 16. This applies with almost double force to the branch of education that concerns itself with sex. The supporting warm relationship in which sexual knowledge is passed and the feelings shared rests on love.

Sex education forms an important part in training a noble Christian character. To be able to make decisions in keeping with such a character requires a knowledge of truth and, unfortunately, sometimes of truth's opposite. Masters and Johnson have pointed out that we can make moral decisions in the area of love only when we know truth.

In sharing truth, parents should gladly give their children more sex education than they themselves received. It is not a case of "what was good enough for me is good enough for you." The world in which your children live keeps moving on at almost breathtaking speed.

If you mix the information with too much and too constant "admonishing" you can generate a form of rebellion. Conscientious or anxious parents need to guard against falling into a pattern of nagging.

On the other hand, a psychologist recently told me that he has dealt with a number of young people who have been so burdened by the desire of their parents to talk about sex that they went out and had sex to get it over with.

Parents are always walking a tightrope: trying to find the balance between too much too soon or too little too late.

Since we are sharing *truth* about sex with our children, we cannot ever lie to them. As they grow older, children have a tendency to forgive parents for many things that they consider unjust, but they thoroughly resent deception. When children are old enough to know that their parents have lied to them about sex, they have to fight feelings of resentment, disillusionment, and lack of trust.

Sometimes half-truths can prove even more jolting than outright lies. No parent must tell all the truth at any one time—even Jesus did not do that—but whatever is told should be true and adapted to the child's level of comprehension.

Some fathers need to guard against trying to force their sons into a too-masculine role—to become a miniature drill sergeant or a young Tarzan of the Apes. Such a pattern may cover up the father's own unconscious feeling of inferiority, and so he pushes his boy too hard by way of compensation. "No one is going to call *my* boy a sissy!"

Incidentally, psychiatrists pretty well agree that "effeminacy" in boys under 7 does not demand immediate professional help. The same is true for girls who exhibit tomboyism in their pre-teen years.

A fair number of American fathers feel quite embarrassed to show affection for their sons. They have been brought up to think that any expression of sentiment between males is a bit on the feminine side and does not reflect the strong, silent male of the species. These same men will likely avoid doing any housework on the assumption that such work is only for women. They hardly understand someone who tells them that nurturance is not inconsistent with masculinity. In fact, their emotional vocabulary can hardly grasp the meaning of the word itself.

"Encourage the expression of love toward God and toward one another. The reason why there are so many hardhearted men and women in the world is that true affection has been regarded as weakness and has been discouraged and repressed. The better nature of these persons was stifled in childhood; and unless the light of divine love shall melt away their cold selfishness, their happiness will be forever ruined. If we wish our children to possess the tender spirit of Jesus and the sympathy that angels manifest for us, we must encourage the generous, loving impulses of childhood."—*The Desire of Ages*, p. 516.

As in any conversation of value, try to be a good listener. The very fact that a child brings a sex question to you indicates a healthy relationship existing between you and him (or her). This kind of trust deserves respect and honest answers. Continued evasion will gradually break down such confidence and either force the child to find answers within himself or from books or peers.

Keep in mind that your children will consider some conversations to be confidential. You may want to ask their permission to share the content with your spouse.

Generally speaking, most adolescents do not feel comfortable talking about sex with their parents. Often they do not perceive their parents as sexual partners and are uncomfortable thinking about their parents' sex relationship. The older parents are in relation to the child, the more he is likely to fantasize that they have no sex life.

A common form of evasion parents resort to is telling the child to wait until he is older. This may work a few times, but finally he begins to understand that he will probably never age fast enough to receive such information.

If you have a child who is unusually slow to ask questions about sex, you may have to engage in gentle pump-priming. If you communicate on other topics regularly, it will not be difficult to include the subject of sex in your day-by-day exchanges. Sexual incidents occurring in the neighborhood or school or church, TV programs on sexual matters, newspaper and magazine articles on such subjects—all can give you a starting point. In some cases you can lead up to a possible conversation about an area of sex by saying, "You know, when I was your age, I used to wonder . . ." or, "When I was your age, I used to be scared of . . ."

Being able to talk freely with you doesn't mean that your child will not want to find out what his own friends would give by way of answers. Communication with you, which provides him with information that keeps him current with other children of his age, will give him a checkpoint for the ideas he picks up from his peers.

Older brothers and sisters often play a large part in the sex education of younger members of the family, sometimes almost filling in as substitute parents. How accurate their information or how wholesome and healthy their view of sex, of course, is often conditioned by your prior frankness and honesty with them.

Open communication on sexual topics will also insure your child against feeling that all the other kids his age know more about the subject than he does. Equality in the possession of information contributes to his self-respect and also furnishes him with protection against exploitation. One cannot afford to be naive in this world. There are always those who enjoy taking advantage of such children.

Remember, when a child asks you questions about sex, he is paying you a compliment. Be sure you listen well enough to know what he is asking. He may ask you where he came from, and after you lecture ten minutes about the facts of life, he may inform you that his friend is from New York.

If he's telling you a story or asking some question, wait until you are sure you understand the whole situation. Jumping to conclusions can lead you down some rough and scary roads.

Don't assume that every question he asks is about himself. And don't go at him as though you were a district attorney with a hostile witness on the stand. Likewise, even though you may be delighted with this opportunity to communicate, don't scare him away by being overeager.

Chapter Thirteen

Sex Play, Vocabulary, and Experimentation

The more wholesome the sex education you provide for your children, the more protective strength they gain from correct knowledge and an informed conscience. This encourages them to resist the impact of lewd and vulgar conversations and improper sexual overtures from peers and adults. Best of all, your children will feel free to report such incidents and matters to you. They will not be afraid that you will misunderstand or scold or shame them.

Your children's associations can also be very significant. Mrs. White points out that one visit to a home where the children practice masturbation can do great harm.

"Neighbors may permit their children to come to your house, to spend the evening and the night with your children. Here is a trial, and a choice for you, to run the risk of offending your neighbors by sending their children to their own home, or gratify them, and let them lodge with your children, and thus expose them to be instructed in that knowledge which would be a life-long curse to them."—*A Solemn Appeal,* p 56.

It is important for you to notice when your children have no curiosity. It is also worthy of your attention if they are too curious. In the latter case, you may have a precocious child, or perhaps a playmate with morbid ideas about sex is forcing him along too fast. Practically all children by the time they reach school age ask where babies come from. When a child does not, you can probably assume that he's had some negative experience that has inhibited a normal curiosity.

Nearing the ages of 6 and 7 boys and girls often think of play situations that require undressing—like playing doctor or "I'll show you mine if you'll show me yours." If a parent comes on the scene when this is happening, he or she should not go into shock or become excited or angry. The children are not trying to be filthy or dirty or abnormal. They are mainly motivated by a legitimate curiosity about sex differences, and these games give them a chance to do some personal research.

Children are also aware of the kind of embarrassed pleasure that they can experience in the process. This awareness is often heightened by their conscious or unconscious feeling that the play really falls in the forbidden zone of behavior. Parents should not deal with these episodes as though they were flagrant violations of morals. Neither should they project on the children their uneasiness and guilt resulting from their own past sexual development. Instead, parents should rule such conduct out of bounds because these are the kinds of games "we don't want you to play." "If you are doing this to learn more about each other's bodies, we shall be glad to show you pictures and explain all you want to know about the differences between fellows and girls." Such an approach puts any later behavior of this kind on the level of disobedience to the parents' orders rather than on the level of shameful and wicked conduct.

Usually by the time children are 6 or 7 their curiosity about the "difference" in sex organs has been satisfied in one way or another. After this age attempts at sex play often reveal the child's need for personal attention in terms of his or her sex development. Of course, elementary caution suggests that children not be allowed to play often or for very long in relative privacy.

Some adults do not share our concern about sex play. A well-known organization in the sex-education field, after stating that children in all cultures "usually seek to engage in sexual-erotic rehearsal play," warns that the prevention or absence of such activity may damage a child's later sex life, even to the point of serious abnormality.

Sex play, in the basic sense of the term, is not primarily sexual. Consider how much difference can exist in the way a pretty, bikini-clad young lady looks to a 5-year-old boy, a teen-age boy, a man of 25, a man of 45, and a man of 75. Children's games that involve the sex organs can often be played with very little real sexual emotions present in the activity. The level of sexual development is only in the budding stage.

Sex education, of course, has its own vocabulary. Many parents feel more comfortable using "baby" terms from the child's early years. Yet we encourage a child to develop a growing vocabulary in other areas of knowledge. Why not, then, do the same regarding sex?

If we do not use the proper names for the organs and their functions, we have to find substitutes. This almost always leads to names that are either silly or degrading or both. They reflect a lack of respect for the dignity and importance of the sex organs and adults' uncomfortableness in referring to them. One of our late presidents, for example, was known for his use of crude names for the penis.

Incidentally, sometimes even the earlier accepted names do not present the organs in attractive terms. For example, the external female organs received the name *pudenda*. This was derived from the Latin word *pudere*, meaning "to be ashamed."

The best way, then, is to use the proper names for the sex organs and for their functions when you talk with your children. If they bring a street word home you can inform them that this is not a proper word to use, and then give them the correct term. Parents ought to get there first with the right words before wrong ones make their impression. A "vaccination" with a good vocabulary is the best protection a child can have in meeting the dirty pictures and words he will see and hear in association with his peers.

In the early years children sometimes use dirty words to shock adults. Very little else they say has such power, and youngsters sometimes find it gratifying to see the effect such language produces. If they continue with such a vocabulary, without correction or help from their parents, when they move into early adolescence they will prove themselves one of the gang by spicing their vocabulary with words that reveal their sexual sophistication. At times, the four (and more) -letter words provide a satisfying form of profanity for young people.

Even in areas totally unconnected with sex, we use sexual terms to describe the function of objects. I have in front of me an advertisement from a horticultural magazine. A company advertising its irrigation system shows illustrations of a "female hose coupling" and a "male hose coupling." Plumbers and electricians, for example, have their own similar trade terms.

One can use animal copulation and animal birth as teaching aids in sex education. Point out, however, the vast difference between that kind of copulation and human intercourse. It is regrettably true that many men often speak of "making love" when they really mean only thc act of copulation. Some do not reach the level of communication and sensitivity that some animals seem to have. Yet, happily married Christian parents can describe the tremendous range of feeling and understanding possible to man and woman in lovemaking. The difference is as great as that between the image of God in man and the brute creation.

Some parents linger too long on the subject of animals. To the children a long way seems to stretch from the animals to man and to themselves. Probably this lingering springs from the parents' nervousness in dealing with the anatomy and psychology of human sexuality, especially as it relates to themselves.

Another indication of our self-consciousness and ambivalence in the matter of sex has been the absence of any real boy dolls for our children. Several years ago there was an attempt to introduce a "little brother" from Europe, but two mothers in Ohio started a campaign against such a shocking action. Many of the adults who have voiced displeasure over the trend toward unisex among adolescents have not had any burden to provide dolls of both sexes for their children. Adults generally take it for granted that children play more wholesomely and safely if their dolls do not suggest the existence of two sexes—at least so far as anatomy is concerned.

Recently a toy manufacturer has begun advertising a boy doll "built exactly the way little boys come into this world." He also "wets when he's full." It will be interesting to see what response this American-made doll will receive from parents and from relatives who purchase dolls for favorite children. Parents who do give these dolls to their children can use them as a comfortable and natural point of departure in sex education. For little girls without a baby brother, they can be particularly appropriate in evoking and satisfying healthy and normal curiosity.

Occasionally, one hears the charge that sex education encourages children into ""sexperimentation." I have not found this to be true from my own experience. In my sex-education classes, I have frequently had the second and third child (and a few times, the fourth and fifth) from the same family. Apparently the parents have found the teaching to be helpful and worthwhile. This would hardly be true if the classes had stimulated the children into experimentation.

As a case in point, in one school where I held sex-education classes the principals have reported a sharp drop in the number of "dirty notes" and graffiti on the restroom walls. When everyone has the same knowledge in the same grade the youngsters have less motivation to show off or to shock.

Dr. R. Eckert, writing in volume 5 of *The Encyclopedia of Mental Health* (1963), stated that "the sex-education programs in Oregon and Wisconsin brought about a significant reduction in illegitimate births, venereal disease and juvenile sex crimes." He said he knew of no research pointing the other way.

Dr. Lester Kirkendall reports in *Sex in the Childhood Years* that, as he helped schools develop sex-education programs, he often heard the fear expressed that sex education would "produce uncontrollable curiosity." To find out whether there could be any basis for this, he did a little survey on his own. He asked 180 boys to indicate the sources of their sex education and to rate them in terms of arousing a kind of "let's-try-it" curiosity. Of boys who received sex education from their fathers, 95 percent said their curiosity had been decreased. Only one boy out of 36 who listed mother as the source reported increased curiosity. School sex education lessened curiosity for 85 percent of the boys. Of 21 who received sex education in a religious setting, none felt any rise in curiosity. However, 96 percent of those who gave friends as their source of information considered that the sex desire increased. Of those who used books and cartoons as sources, 93 percent reported excitement. Dr. Kirkendall concluded: "*This is convincing proof that the way sex education is given rather than the mere mention of sex is the thing with which to be concerned.*"—Pages 30, 31.

The American Medical Association's Committee on Human Sexuality has concluded: "Considerable evidence indicates that sexual knowledge tends to reduce the likelihood of undesirable sexual behavior and experimentation caused by curiosity."—*Human Sexuality*, p. 35.

Because parents have assumed that the children receiving sex education might "want to go out and try it," they have provided little or no sex education. They have assumed that ignorance will preserve the child's innocence. Yet the very young people who are the least informed about sex in a positive way are those most actively involved in it.

Ignorance may appear to preserve a child's sexual purity, but protective knowledge properly transmitted is still safer—both spiritually and morally. Ever since Adam and Eve ate from the forbidden tree, the members of their family have had to distinguish between good and evil knowledge.

Chapter Fourteen

Molestation

We come now to a very painful and distasteful subject. However, I would not be frank and honest to write a book about sex education without including some discussion of molestation. (Incidentally, a family member who engages in molestation most likely will not buy this book.)

Statistics indicate that one out of three or four girls will be victims of some form of molestation in their preadult years. The great majority of such experiences for girls will either involve exhibitionism or fondling of the genital organs. For boys the majority of contacts are made by either homosexuals or immature heterosexual adults. Rarely do older women seduce boys. Keep in mind that there is no standard situation. No two relationships or sets of consequences are alike.

Frederic Storaska, in his book *How to Say No to a Rapist and Survive,* writes: "It is almost certain that at least once in your life you will be the victim of a 'minor' sexual annoyance" "from an obscene phone call, frottage, an exhibitionist, or a peeping tom."—Chapter 12. (*Frottage* is not a common term. It means that a man gets sexual stimulation by rubbing against a girl's body, as can occur in a crowded elevator or railroad car.) As any parent might guess, about 90 percent of the molesters are men.

Some of you, perhaps, can recall an episode or two in your own lives. Time and maturity have dimmed their impact, but you can still recall the shock and disgust aroused by such experiences.

Fortunately, molesters rarely use physical force. Most of the time the molester is someone the child knows. A large number of such acts involve family members, neighbors, or acquaintances of the child. Many such experiences are likely to occur in the girl's home. Naturally, the child is often told not to tell, and the molester threatens the youngster with unpleasant consequences or maybe offers a bribe of some gift or favor.

How can parents explain molestation to a child in such a way as to protect her (assume "him" also from here on) without causing too great revulsion or crippling fear? Point out such things as the following: The molester feels inadequate to relate to adult women and so does such things to make himself feel more like a man; he is basically not "grown-up"; he certainly does not understand the private quality of sex; these experiences give him a temporary feeling of importance, which is increased by his victim's wide-eyed fright and shocked awareness of what he is doing or saying. The younger the child, the simpler the explanation; even to the point of saying that the molester "should not be doing *that*."

Incidentally, when molesters end up in prison for such offenses, they usually find themselves at the bottom of the "social register" among the inmates. They are in a sense failures even among failures.

In cases involving ordinary types of molestation, evidence suggests that the long-range consequences to the victim are relatively mild. In some cases serious effects do occur, but parents should not assume that tragic consequences always will follow. One child psychiatrist reports seeing many children who have suffered no such detrimental effects on their personalities.

Often a case of child molesting will shock the parents more than it does the child. Unfortunately, the reaction of the parents can widen and deepen any scars left. Of course, the child's recovery from such an experience depends largely on her emotional health and how well and wisely her affectional needs are being met.

The most difficult cases of molestation occur within the family or the circle of relatives. Sometimes a mother is aware of previous misconduct on the part of a male yet still allows him to be alone with her daughter. If the girl finds out about an earlier episode and her mother's knowledge of it, she can lose a lot of faith in her mother's judgment and question just how deep her love is.

The most serious offense in the home is, of course, a sexual relation between a parent and child—usually father or stepfather and daughter. Grandfathers are also occasional offenders. Once in a while a brother or uncle is the culprit. In one study of female psychiatric patients involved in incest, the relationships were found to have gone on for an average of eight years. (Surprising as it may seem, mothers in such cases are often conscious of what is going on, even though they may not permit themselves to face up to the real situation.)

Sometimes the father will justify the relationship as a way of teaching his daughter about sex. In discipline he spanks his daughter and then appears to ease the pain by caressing and fondling her in a questionable manner.

When a child has not had a normal amount of loving and emotional security, she is more likely to interpret these sexual overtures as a mark of affection and so respond to them because of her deprivation and hunger. Her response, however, should not be considered to be sexual. She is too young to respond as a mature sexual person. She accepts the attentions and enjoys her ability to pay for them. She also feels flattered by such treatment from an older person. If the offender is her father or stepfather, she may feel an immature kind of pride in usurping her mother's place.

Dr. Joyce Brothers, in a recent column, wrote that "it would be hard to exaggerate the damage that incestuous relations have on a child." Incest can and often does cause serious emotional effects. Whether there will be serious long-term effects on the girl who is the victim ("willing" or otherwise) depends on a number of related factors: the "repairs" made in the sex education of the girl, the emotional climate of the home after the revelation, and whether there will be social and legal treatment of the male offender.

Of girls victimized by their fathers some later function quite well as women. Others, however, have trouble in their sex lives. This is evident, for example, from a question turned in during a camp meeting session: "Any suggestions for a girl who has been sexually mistreated by her father since she was little? Now it is affecting her physical relationship with her husband. She doesn't like kissing and has an almost zero sex drive."

Keeping the channels of communication open with our children in terms of sex makes it easier for them to report an act of molestation. (Basically, keeping the channel open provides the key to *all* sex education.) Often those who are victims of this type of mistreatment try to put the incident out of mind and wall it off from their consciousness. This attempt can be intensified by a feeling of guilt. Although they may have done nothing to cause this molestation, they can easily assume that in some way, unknown to them, they somehow brought such treatment on themselves.

Contemporary leniency in sexual matters offers another outstanding evidence of the decline in moral standards during the past few decades. A recent full-page article in *Time* reported that a number of researchers maintain that adult-child sex "is basically harmless to the child." One sexologist says that incest "can sometimes be beneficial." Another is quoted as stating that " 'It is almost certain that human beings, like the other primates, require a period of early sexual rehearsal play.' " A psychologist takes the position that no one is harmed by adult-child sex " 'so long as it occurs in a relationship with somebody who really cares about the child.' " (Two psychiatrists and a psychotherapist strongly oppose these conclusions.)

The psychotherapist referred to is Dr. Sam Janus, whose book *The Death of Innocence* appeared in 1981. He reports shocking data on teen sex, incest, sexual exploitation of children, teen prostitution, and pornography involving children and teens. One authority, for example, he quotes as saying that "incest is widespread in America."

The saddest chapter title, in my opinion, is "Children No More." The most encouraging statement, based on a study of 2,795 females is, again in my opinion, "The *sexually inactive* [italics in the original] girls attend religious schools, where no pregnancies have been reported in the past ten years and where drug use is uncommon."

Fortunately, most parents will never have to deal with the rape of a daughter. Nevertheless, a few comments may be in order. Sometimes the experience can cause a long-lasting emotional "abscess" that never is totally drained and healed. Or in the words of one sociologist, it may be equivalent to an emotional time bomb.

Parents' fears and wrong ideas about rape can often intensify and prolong the effects. The horror and distress that some people show can indelibly mark the victim for life. A girl's loss of virginity in rape can be treated as an irreversible stigma. Reassuring support is a must for the young woman to maintain emotional balance.

Parents of victims naturally feel anger and revulsion. The father may threaten to kill the man. Girls often judge the seriousness of the situation by the kind of emotions the encounter stirs up. Again, it must be pointed out that the young girl cannot experience intercourse, especially in rape, in the same way as an adult, and therefore should not be the object of feelings arising from an adult perception of the assault.

Some communities offer services to help rape victims (or victims of any form of molestation). The staff members are trained to understand and give support. Probably most initial contacts are made in hospital emergency rooms. Such staff members can also help a boyfriend, fiancé, or husband relate to the attack in a way that can relieve the victim's shame and sense of degradation.

To protect your child—as far as possible—from molestation, warn the younger children:

1. To run away from strangers who offer food, toys, candy, or a ride or who say they were sent by Daddy or Mommy.

2. To stay away from alleys, empty buildings, bushy areas, strange houses, garages, and sheds. (If alleys are the only place to play—a sad situation— then be sure to play with a group.)

3. To stay in approved playgrounds that you have selected.

4. To tell you always where they are going.

5. To report at once any improper behavior. They are to be young Christians, of course, but in matters such as this, kindness is misplaced, and it is not "telling" on someone to report such overtures. Another child may be protected from a later attempt if such a person is quickly

apprehended. The man may threaten the child with harm if she tells, but such threats, fortunately, are rarely carried out. Tell your child *never* to say, "I'm going to tell my mother." (This *can* invite killing.)

6. To be aware that any caressing or asking for caresses or touching of the genital areas is a sick way to behave. One author calls molesters "friend-sick" people. This is both clever and kind and will protect your daughter from feeling besmirched by any approaches that may have been made before she realized that something was wrong.

7. To show extra caution (such as taking a friend along) when using some park and public playground restrooms.

8. To avoid wandering off by themselves when out with a group.

9. To refrain from entering a stranger's home.

10. To refuse strangers admittance to your home when you are away, no matter what story they tell about being friends of the family.

Warn your older daughters:

1. To stay in well-lighted areas as much as possible when out at night.

2. To arrange for escorting by father or brother to any place at night if a dependable male friend will not accompany her.

3. To avoid "blind dates" and accept them only when they include a reliable couple, or friends.

4. To avoid "parking" in secluded places, especially those known to be favored by young people.

5. To avoid dressing or acting in any way that might be considered provocative.

6. To walk confidently, directly, and steadily when alone.

7. To walk on the side of the street facing traffic.

8. To avoid walking close to doorways, bushes, and

alleys where a rapist might hide.

9. To be careful when people stop and ask for directions—never get too close to the car.

10. To scream and run if danger appears imminent.

11. To scream for help or yell "Fire!" if in trouble.

12. To accept a ride only from women or older couples—never from single men or boisterous groups.

13. To lock all the car doors at *all* times.

14. To park the car only in well-lighted areas.

15. To check the back seat of a parked car before getting inside.

16. To drive to a public place or a police station when being followed.

17. To open the hood of the car and attach a white cloth to the antenna if her car breaks down and to stay inside the locked car if someone stops to help and to ask the "good Samaritan" to call the police or a garage.

In general, train your children to be alert but not always fearful. They can learn to recognize certain tip-offs that should ring an alarm. You, in turn, will notice with extra care any friends or relatives who seem to show inappropriate attentions to your girl or boy. Be especially on guard when a child is reluctant to tell you where he or she went or what occurred during this time. Keep molestation in mind as a possible cause of sudden nightmares, sleepwalking, loss of appetite, and sudden insistence on privacy.

Incest indicates an unhealthy relationship between the father and the mother. When these cases come to the attention of the church, discipline should include professional help for both parents.

In fairness to innocent people, check to make sure that any story told you of molestation is not a fabrication on the part of your child. Children seldom dream up such charges, but the possibility must be kept in mind. Some fine persons have been ruined because of untrue accusations.

Of course, none of what has been suggested here about molestation can be properly conveyed to your children unless they have had sex education appropriate to their level of development. Such education and the relationship that it implies are in themselves a basic form of prevention against incidents. And when incidents occur—as they sometimes do—provide a healthy setting in which to *avoid or minimize any possible damaging effects.*

Chapter Fifteen

Masturbation

Masturbation is one of the least-talked-about subjects among us, and it is potentially one of the most controversial, especially as it concerns the integrity of the Ellen G. White writings. Some feel that in this area the thinking of her times heavily influenced her. (It is true that much of what she has written on the subject of masturbation cannot be proved from medicine—especially psychiatry—and psychology and is quite contrary to what intelligent and informed people today accept as rational and logical.) Therefore, these Adventists have concluded that a traditional but totally wrong philosophy (contemporary with her) has somehow crept into the overwhelming mass of fine writing that otherwise fills her books.

It should be noted, too, that it would also be unusual to find an exception to modern secular opinion regarding masturbation among the leaders of the main-line denominations. The Roman Catholic Church stands adamantly against masturbation, considering it (when not a symptom of emotional illness) a mortal sin. However, there is very little in their condemnation of the practice that includes the great variety of unhappy physical consequences mentioned by Ellen G. White.

In my former book, *God Invented Sex,* I quoted

extensively from her writings on this subject. Since most Adventists do not have a copy of *A Solemn Appeal,* which deals primarily with the subject of masturbation, I quoted a few excerpts from it. Much more comes from the second and fourth volumes of *Testimonies for the Church,* plus *Healthful Living,* and *Medical Ministry.* This is followed by quotations from Dr. J. H. Kellogg's *Man, the Masterpiece* or *Plain Truths Plainly Told, About Boyhood, Youth and Manhood.* Finally I reproduced the treatment of this subject from a phrenologist of that period, whose writing appears quite similar in content to what Ellen White wrote.

To find the references in their full setting, you can look up the subject in your *Comprehensive Index to the Writings of Ellen G. White* under "self-abuse; vice." If you don't have the *Index,* look in the indexes of the two volumes of the *Testimonies* referred to, under the subject heading, "Vice, secret." (See also *Child Guidance,* pp. 434-468.)

After having presented the positions of Jewish relgious leaders of the past, authorities in the field of sex and sex education today, and current thinking in branches of the modern religious world, I concluded by saying: "As a people we point out how reliable and trustworthy her counsel was and is, especially when she saw ahead to discoveries only recently made. Time after time we have seen her statements vindicated, even when out of harmony with the medical and psychological opinion of her day. They include the relationship between faulty diet and juvenile delinquency, the beneficial effect of sunlight, dangers in the excessive use of salt, the presence of animal fats or sugar in helping to produce blood-vessel diseases, the value of walking as an exercise, the dangers of hypnosis as a 'mind cure,' risks of misuse of X-ray, the tremendous importance of psychosomatic medicine, the relation between stress and longevity, the powers of prenatal influence, the statement that 'germs' are a causative factor in cancer, the destructive power of tobacco, and the relation between drugs and birth defects."—Page 164.

Then I end on this note: "If we think she is wrong about masturbation, we had better reexamine our understanding of the operation of prophecy in the church. If we feel that she is right, we need to act on what she wrote, pending eventual confirmation."—Page 164.

"Our denomination needs a conference at the top level on sex and marriage, participated in by physicians, behavioral scientists, and theologians. Such a group could prepare at least a tentative theology of sex. And such a theology could indicate where harmony exists between Mrs. White's writings and the general thinking of the world at large, and where we find irreconcilable opposition. The latter position would, of necessity, have to have a basis on a sound interpretation of the Scriptures, Ellen G. White's writings, and incontestable medical data."— Page 165.

As many of you know, Ronald L. Numbers in his book, *Prophetess of Health,* raises serious questions about Mrs. White's writings in the field of health. Among the subjects dealt with was that of masturbation. The author clearly implies that her statements about the many negative consequences of the practice were merely borrowed from contemporary physicians.

In their response to the book, the Ellen G. White Estate, the official custodians of her writings, state "that this is one of the few areas of her teachings which has not yet been sustained by scientific studies."—*A Critique of Prophetess of Health,* p. 72.

They then add: "An experienced psychologist, Dr. Elden Chalmers of Andrews University, who has done a great deal of careful study in this field, reports that as he has made inquiry of recognized authorities in this field, the authors who have made mention of masturbation in their writings on the subject when pressed, have admitted that sound evidence is not available. No longitudinal studies have been concluded in this area. On the other hand, he declares that there has not yet been found evidence which would disprove Ellen G. White's teaching on masturbation or sex."

The custodians conclude: "In the case of masturbation, we believe that it could well be that in time her statement will be supported. Who knows what the investigations of another decade or two may yield? But even if it were not, those who believe that Ellen White did not lie, when she said she 'saw' will be content to maintain suspended judgment."—*Ibid.*, p. 73.

On this subject I take my stand with the brethren in the White Estate. The reference in the quotation from the White Estate mentions that she "saw." Here are some statements on this nature I have collected. She made all of them in reference to masturbation.

"Many cases have been presented before me, and as I have had a view of their inner lives, my soul has been sick and disgusted with the rotten-heartedness of human beings who profess godliness and talk of translation to heaven."—*Testimonies*, vol. 2, p. 349.

"The Lord has given me a view of some of the corruptions everywhere existing."—*Ibid.*, p. 390.

"I saw that the family of Brother ______ need a great work done for them. ______ and ______ have gone to great lengths in this crime of self-abuse."—*Ibid.*, p. 404.

"I have been shown that persons of apparently good deportment, not taking unwarrantable liberties with the other sex, were guilty of practicing secret vice nearly every day of their lives. They have not refrained from this terrible sin even while most solemn meetings have been in session."—*Ibid.*, p. 469.

Other statements about masturbation imply indirectly that the information came from special revelation:

"Your children have practiced self-abuse."—*Ibid.*, p. 392.

"I might mention the cases of many others."—*Ibid.*, p. 406.

"Self-abuse is practiced by him."—*Ibid.*, p. 408.

"There are many more cases I might designate, but I have named enough already. Young girls are not as a general thing clear of the crime of self-abuse."—*Ibid.*, p. 409.

"Chapter after chapter has been opened to me. I can select family after family of children in this house, every one of whom is as corrupt as hell itself."—*Ibid.*, p. 360. (Note the exceptional severity of this language.)

Since she was writing about what she terms "solitary vice," she had no other way of securing her knowledge except by direct enlightenment of her mind.

One particular case deserves mention. It appears in *Child Guidance*, beginning on page 450. She relates that her husband and she attended a meeting where a member of the church was a great sufferer "with the phthisic." The brethren met at his house and had prayer for him, and the Whites were asked to pray for him.

However, she says that she "had resolved not to engage in prayer for anyone, unless the Spirit of the Lord should dictate in the matter." That night she and her husband asked the Lord whether they should pray for him. The Lord showed them in a dream that He would not hear such a prayer because the man "regarded iniquity in his heart." The iniquity? Practicing masturbation from his early years and continuing it in his married life (he was now in middle age). Ellen White saw that he was debasing himself daily, yet asking God for "an increase of strength which he had vilely squandered."

One particular statement stands out in her report of

this case. "This vice was shown me as an abomination in the sight of God." You will recall that the word *abomination* is used in Leviticus 18 of adultery, homosexuality, bestiality, and intercourse during menstruation.

The church needs to examine closely her counsel on masturbation. "There are but few professed Christians," she wrote, "who regard this matter in the right light and who hold proper government over themselves when public opinion and custom do not condemn them."—*Testimonies*, vol. 2, p. 348.

"When persons are addicted to the habit of self-abuse, it is impossible to arouse their sensibilities to appreciate eternal things, or to delight in spiritual exercises."—*Ibid.*, p. 470. Our age is marked with teeming corruption, and licentiousness is its special sin. Paul's dreadful description in Romans 1 applies to our world at his time.—*Child Guidance*, pp. 439, 440. And in such a setting Satan's special work is "to take possession of the minds of youth."—*Ibid.*

In my opinion no other sin does Ellen G. White so strongly denounce. Notice the expressions she uses in speaking of it: debasing, soul-and-body-destroying indulgence (*Testimonies*, vol. 2, p. 470); vicious practice (*ibid.*, p. 402); corrupting vice (*ibid.*); hellish practice (*ibid.*, p. 403); awful crime (*ibid.*, p. 469); degrading vice (*ibid.*, p. 347); soul-and-body-destroying vice (*ibid.*). Most surprisingly, she says that moral pollution (in this context masturbation) has done more than every other evil to cause the race to degenerate (*ibid.*, p. 391). The habit, she states, "leads to fornication and adultery."—*A Solemn Appeal*, p. 53.

Even a casual reading of her writings reveals her belief, as God's messenger, that masturbation can damage the eyes, nose, muscles, liver, kidneys, back, spine, and nerves. She states that it can bring on rheumatism, neuralgia, palpitation, enfeeblement, decay, dropsy; in fact, diseases of almost every description. It can disturb the functioning of the brain, intellect, memory, and imagination. It can damage the personality. The spiritual nature can be made impervious to heavenly appeals, and the image of God can gradually be destroyed.

One statement from her writings mentions the habit among adolescents. "Children who practice self-indulgence previous to puberty, or the period of merging into manhood or womanhood, must pay the penalty of nature's violated laws at that critical period. . . . If the practice is continued from the age of fifteen and upward, nature will protest against the abuse she has suffered, and continues to suffer, and will make them pay the penalty for the transgression of her laws, especially from the ages of thirty to forty-five, by numerous pains in the system, and various diseases . . . and cancerous humours. Some of nature's fine machinery gives way, leaving a heavier task for the remaining to perform, which disorders nature's fine arrangement, and there is often a sudden breaking down of the constitution; and death is the result."—*Ibid.* pp. 63, 64.

At present, to my knowledge, no generally recognized medical evidence supports these indictments. In fact, the evidence appears to go contrary to her list of problems caused by masturbation.

If I were to guess why she denounces the habit so soundly, I would reason along these lines. Masturbation violates the basic purpose of the genital organs. They were designed to produce one-fleshness. This, in turn, was a part of the image of God in man. One-fleshness probably symbolized on a creature level the nearest relationship that approximates the intimacy of the three Persons of the Trinity.

When young persons masturbate, they direct their sexual drive inward—in effect they make love to themselves, or more accurately they copulate with themselves. The pleasure and thrill derived from ejaculation become only part of a self-pleasing activity. (Incidentally, one of the modern terms for masturbation is *self-pleasuring.)* If this is accompanied with fantasies of women, in which the masturbator either forces himself on them or receives their willing response, the intent of the act is further weakened. These fantasies prostitute the real reciprocal relationship in which the act of intercourse becomes the method of achieving one-fleshness.

On the other hand, those who accept the theory of evolution can have an attitude that is completely different. For them the body is the product of a long process of evolution. The sexual differentiation and physical and emotional sexuality are refinements gained by the human branch of the animal kingdom.

Other animals in their view have made progress as well, but the "naked ape" has arrived at the highest level of refinement and complexity. Throughout this long, ongoing progress there has been, for man, no creating or sustaining God, no Lawgiver, no fall of man, no sin, and no necessity for a Saviour. Man is, in essence, a highly developed animal and nothing more. Mankind creates its own laws and social practices and is not answerable to any Creator-God for conduct.

For such a man (or woman), masturbation is a necessary and natural outlet for the sex drive, a welcome form of relief from sexual tension. These people feel they can practice it all through life, the frequency and intensity governed by conditions at any given time. If they are married, they will resort to it when lovemaking between husband and wife is not possible.

They regard it as a natural function and separate it entirely from any relationship in which the act of ejaculation is part of the expression of one-fleshness. The act, to a large degree, becomes an end in itself.

Such people have the insensitivity of those described in Romans 1. They identify closely with their supposed earlier animal ancestors or with their current animal neighbors. They can engage in such acts with the mindlessness of animals.

Perhaps the Lord's repugnance and anger springs from His displeasure over any act that makes a travesty of what He intended in the Creation of Adam and Eve as sexual beings. Since this is such a violation of His purposes, perhaps there is some built-in curse on the physical, emotional, and mental natures of those who engage in masturbation. There is doubtless much to learn in the area of psychophysiological disease. We generally pay a price in sickness and weakness when we violate the integrity of our bodies and subject them to unhealthful practices. Perhaps the same thing occurs in masturbation, but we do not yet perceive the cause-and-effect relationship. After all, relatively little study has been done on the possible physical and emotional dangers of masturbation.

Harder still, of course, is how to measure the destruction of the soul, which Mrs. White so often mentions and describes. How can masturbation bring this about? Does it steadily profane the image of God? Does it produce a steady loss of sensitivity as to the meaning of human sexuality as God purposed it? Does its solitariness clearly contradict the intent of one-fleshness—of the total communion of man and woman? Does it destroy the analogy with the relationship of the Persons of the Trinity, who are incapable of any self-serving acts? Does man in this practice "animalize" or "de-soul" himself? I don't know.

Now back to parents and children.

Ellen White mourned for the young who were forming characters in this degenerate age. (Keep in mind that she wrote during an earlier century.) Her distress was not confined to the dangers facing youth. "I tremble for their parents also," she wrote.—*Testimonies,* vol. 2, p. 348. She felt it is a crime for mothers to remain ignorant in regard to the habits of their children.—See *A Solemn Appeal,* p. 58. This lack of alertness she charges up to Satan, who has "paralyzed" the minds of parents.—*Testimonies,* vol. 2, p. 481.

"Many [children] might have been saved if they had been carefully instructed in regard to the influence of this practice upon their health."—*Child Guidance,* p. 457. "If you have not instructed them in regard to the violation of the laws of health, blame rests upon you."—*Ibid.,* pp. 458, 459. "Fortify their young minds, and prepare them to detest this health-and-soul destroying vice."—*Ibid.,* p. 457.

From these statements I infer that children should receive basic sex education. Surely she could not assume that parents teach their children the evils of masturbation as a subject by itself, divorcing it from a sound Christian theology of sex. Evidently, too, she thought it wise to bring this subject to the attention of children in their early years, suited, of course, to the child's level of understanding and his particular type of personality. One can't condemn masturbation in a void. Detached from the framework of Christian sex, outcries against masturbation have no significance. The whole thrust of our education in this area should be to help children see that "it is God, the pure and holy God, that they have been sinning against."—*Child Guidance,* p. 459.

How should parents deal with masturbation? She urges them to ask the Lord for wisdom and to engage often in fervent prayer. She advises them that one rule cannot be applied in every case. Parents must have sanctified judgment. They should not be censorious or agitated or hasty. Such approaches can bring on unnecessary rebellion in their children.

In addition to educating the children on the subject of sex and the evils of practicing masturbation, she offers some advice in prevention. To avoid the possibility of her children's learning the habit from friends, she did not allow her children to sleep together in the same bed or in the same room. She did not permit neighbor children to spend the night at her home, even though other parents might feel offended.—*A Solemn Appeal*, p. 56.

A statement on the gift of prophecy was adopted at the General Conference session in April, 1980. Included are these significant words: "Her writings are a continuing and authoritative source of truth and provide for the church, comfort, guidance, instruction, and correction."

We need to be aware that psychiatrists, psychologists, sex educators, sex therapists, and other professionals working in the area of sex generally hold a different perspective on masturbation. They usually agree that masturbation is beneficial, healthy, and normal.

A survey of current literature will reveal such ideas as the following:

There is no clinical evidence that masturbation ever injures a person's health.

Masturbation may have important positive benefits: It helps young people know themselves better as sexual persons and understand the sensations possible from stimulation of the sex organs.

Masturbation is a good substitute practice for sexual intercourse while a young person matures emotionally enough for a sexual relationship.

Women who engage in masturbation are more responsive in sexual relations. In fact, evidence shows that women with a higher-than-average frequency of orgasms in intercourse are those who have masturbated regularly.

Masturbation not only relieves sexual tension, but it also provides a release for tensions originating in nonsexual areas.

Masturbation can help a person overcome sexual inadequacy.

In masturbation excess is nearly impossible.

Boys who masturbate probably are "better balanced" than those who feel compelled to abstain or who masturbate chronically.

Abstaining from masturbation when there is no heterosexual outlet arouses the suspicion that the abstinence is neurotic.

Guilt feelings about masturbation can cause psychosomatic illness.

Masturbation is the normal response to an increased sexual drive and serves to control and integrate these new urges.

The Christian community is starting to affirm masturbation as a healthy kind of sexual activity. One minister-author calls it a "gift of God."

Those who masturbate avoid some of the problems that result from sexual intercourse.

Some religious ideas and ideals lead to guilt feelings about masturbation and consequent repression.

"Good mothering" will lead to the development of masturbation in infancy.

Perhaps some Seventh-day Adventist psychiatrists and psychologists share some of the above ideas. I do not state this as an accusation of heresy. I respect their right to interpret Ellen G. White's writing on the subject in whatever way they choose so as to avoid conflict with what they consider truth in their own field of medicine. These individuals feel that in some cases we should consider masturbation acceptable and beneficial. They do not equate masturbation under certain specific conditions with self-abuse. For example, in the case of two spouses who are separated for a long time but who fantasize of each other during the act. Or they may think that masturbation can provide a healthy release for a widow or widower who enjoyed a happy marriage with a deeply satisfying sex relationship but who now finds himself or herself deprived of this part of life.

Other Adventist psychologists, teachers, and doctors feel they have found satisfactory support for Ellen White's counsel on masturbation. The evidence they point to is usually only partial, however, and does not buttress her warnings of the many physical ills she said masturbation causes.

Perhaps the time has come for an Adventist organization to collect and evaluate such information. Because the subject is distasteful, we can easily avoid researching the matter. However, since Ellen White so outspokenly condemns masturbation, we owe it to ourselves and all future converts to leave no stone unturned in investigating supportive—and nonsupportive—evidence.

If you want help in dealing with a masturbating son or daughter, please read the section on "Suggestions on Dealing With Masturbation" in *Teens and Love and Sex.* By working out a parallel list from the parental point of view, you can probably find some assistance in how to approach the problem.

Chapter Sixteen

Homosexuality

Practically all of us have encountered such words as *queers, fairies, faggots,* and *gays*—common terms for the male homosexual. Probably the most common term for the female homosexual is *lesbian.*

Despite much current research, no one cause of homosexuality has been isolated to the satisfaction of all behavioral scientists. Some authorities think that parents play a primary role in the development of such an orientation. As I mentioned in *God Invented Sex,* the father is often credited as the key figure in this process. He may show hostile feelings, he may have little to do with his son, or he may be a weak and ineffectual male figure. On the other hand, the mother may be too intimate with her son, tying him to her with strong emotional cords. She may favor him, giving him more attention than mothers normally do, and may sometimes be closer to him than she is to her husband.

Some studies of the mothers of lesbian daughters show these mothers as being critical of their daughters and preventing them from engaging in normal feminine activities in the home. These mothers have tended to defeminize their daughters and have often kept them from developing normal relationships with males.

The fathers of lesbians have supposedly not provided

suitable male models for their daughters. They often dominate and emotionally seduce the girls. Frequently they subtly compete with their daughter's young male friends. Such fathers often cherish strict but unhealthy views of sex and thereby prevent their daughters from developing a normal sexual maturity. One psychiatrist has gone so far as to say that "paternal love can avert homosexuality."

Dr. L. S. Hatterer, who has treated over 800 male homosexuals, says, "I have never known a family yet where love, acceptance, and open communication prevailed that turned out a totally committed homosexual."—*God Invented Sex*, p. 180.

On the other hand, Dr. Ray B. Evans, associate professor of psychiatry at Loma Linda University, suggests that the evidence indicates that the fathers and mothers of some homosexuals had as good relations with their children as have the parents of heterosexuals. —*God Invented Sex*, p. 179.

D. Wardell Pomeroy, a recognized authority on sex, has stated that environmental factors can influence children. According to his view, parents have "only limited control" over the way in which their children will turn out sexually.

Troy Perry, pastor and founder of the original Metropolitan Community Church—for homosexuals—indicates in his autobiography that his relations with his parents were normal. (See *God Invented Sex*, p. 178.)

Other authorities regard homosexuality as a product of sexual development that has been stalled at an immature level; others see an underlying biological tendency; some consider it a personality pattern reaction; others view it as a "maldevelopment"; while yet others think homosexuality is a symptom of a deep-rooted personality disorder. These suggestions simply increase the confusion about the real genesis of homosexuality. We just don't know what causes it.

The male homosexual is not easy to identify at first. Over 90 percent do not look or act like the stereotyped figures most of us envision when we hear the word *homosexual.* Only a small percentage—those prone to swishy ways or who wear a style of clothing preferred by homosexual "in" groups are easily picked out. (Incidentaly, gays sometimes lead out in introducing new styles to the heterosexual world.) One young homosexual told me candidly that he was working on his wrist action and his way of walking, to avoid drawing attention to himself.

The majority of homosexuals engage in sex freely and often. Some, however, develop relationships that resemble heterosexual marriages. These partners will live together for years

Persons who transfer into a job or profession that is almost exclusively filled by the other sex are sometimes considered to be homosexual. For example, a woman mechanic or a female driver of heavy machinery; a male dancer or hairdresser. A number of people assume that all homosexuals are antagonistic to the opposite sex or that they will likely seduce children into their way of life. These ideas are largely mythical.

However, one recent case in my own State of North Carolina, as reported in *The Charlotte Observer,* points up the need for parental alertness. A coach whom boys greatly admired was accused of engaging in sexual acts with 13 boys. The man in question had never been seen having dates with women, but he always had a group of boys surrounding him. He particularly favored blond fellows between 9 and 14. To some he gave money; to others, gifts. He even took some of the fellows to religious services. After he had engaged with them in sex acts, he would warn them that it would be a sin to reveal their behavior to anyone. In a period of three or four months, he was involved in 62 sexual contacts.

As you would expect, it was very difficult to get the boys to talk about what had happened. The parents, when they found out about it, were "reluctant at first to let their sons testify, fearing they would be called homosexuals and psychologically harmed." Later, the parents changed their minds and decided to prosecute.

In fairness, it should be stated that such conduct on the part of an adult homosexual probably occurs less frequently than does the molestation of girls by heterosexuals. Nevertheless, it behooves parents to be aware.

A certain amount of sex play with members of the same sex does not indicate, by itself, that a child is on the road to adult homosexuality. Boys, for example, in the early years of staying exclusively within their own sex group, may look at and sometimes touch another boy's sex organs, usually under the cover of a rough game. They are merely revealing their curiosity about the genitals. Two or more youngsters may sometimes engage in masturbation. They may decide that the distance the ejaculate can shoot measures masculinity.

Occasionally, adolescents form strong attachments to older persons of the same sex. This hero worship does not, in and of itself, indicate any leaning toward homosexual preference. However, a boy's frequent and intense crushlike relations with other boys may indicate a problem.

Even "sissified" behavior should not, by itself, make parents fear that their son is destined to become a homosexual. Some fellows generally show masculine behavior but go in for more refined activities such as music and reading, rather than for contact sports. Vice versa, a number of "tough guys" have gone in for needlework without any loss of respect for their maleness, especially when the person involved is a nationally known football player.

If you do have any serious question as to whether your child shows early signs of homosexuality, consult with a child psychologist or a psychiatrist, preferably one of your own faith or with an evangelical persuasion.

Worry about a child who might be homosexual is probably the worst anxiety parents can experience. Sometimes this heavy emotional burden seems more than the parents can bear. Parents often wrestle with shame and feelings of possible guilt. One mother said of her daughter, who lived with a homosexual teacher, "I'd rather have her come home pregnant than to know she's a homosexual."

Young people, too, can worry about homosexuality. Dr. S. M. Woods, director of Student Psychiatric Services in the University of Southern California at Los Angeles, believes that any failure to adapt in life can be seen unconsciously by the fellow involved as a failure to be a man. These feelings can readily lead to a fear of being a homosexual. Dr. Woods puts the sequence like this: "I am a failure. . . . I am not a man. . . . I am like a woman. . . . I am a homosexual."

Ann Landers tells parents who have learned that their children are gay that "this isn't the end of the world." She points out that many homosexuals enjoy life and don't want to change. Since the child has no desire to become heterosexual, the responsibility for change, she says, rests on the parents. They need to change *their* attitude.

The major problem is, of course, how Christians should classify homosexuality. Is it all sin, all sickness, a mixture of both, or just a different way of life?

Many homosexuals resent being classified as sick. They feel that they have exercised a personal right and have chosen a different style of sexual behavior. They insist that they have not been motivated by sick or unhealthy conditions in their environment or in their personalities.

One young woman homosexual wrote *Time* a letter of protest (3-13-78) and closed with the statement: "Life could have certainly handed me a lot worse things than being a lesbian—I could have become a psychiatrist." (I write this with apologies to my psychiatrist friends.)

The Scriptures, however, condemn the practice categorically—for example: Genesis 19; Leviticus 18:22; Judges 19; Romans 1; 1 Corinthians 6:9, 10.

The editor of *Christianity Today* (4-18-80) stated the evangelical position without reservation: "The plain teaching of Scripture is that all homosexual activity is sinful."

Today we see the "very sins . . . which were in Sodom"—the *SDA Bible Commentary*, Ellen G. White comments, on vol. 4, p. 1,161), and "our world is becoming a second Sodom."—*Child Guidance*, p. 441. These sins exist even among "some who profess to be looking for the coming of the Son of man."—*Testimonies*, vol. 5, p. 218.

Dr. Jack Provonsha, in an article entitled "The Christian, Homosexuals and the Law" (*Spectrum*, vol. 9, no. 2), cautions (and I agree with him): "The thoughtful Christian is also committed to the conviction that no one should be blamed, condemned or even looked down upon for something over which he has no control. . . . And the Christian knows, if he is informed, that a homosexual may not have chosen to be a homosexual. At least for some homosexuals, their condition is something they discover rather than choose."

Some researchers in human sexuality reason that since a person's sexual orientation is determined before the tenth year, neither heterosexuality nor homosexuality is a decision "capable of being made consciously by a person." As one woman wrote: "I have been a lesbian from the day I was born."

You will, of course, protect your child, as far as possible, against molestation. This will most often involve a man and your daughter. But parents also have to allow for the possibility of a man-boy approach. Probably it is best to leave a specific explanation of homosexuality until the early teen years—depending, of course, on the level of sophistication of the children in your social group. Explain that conservative Christians regard homosexuality as both a sin and a warping of God's original purpose in creating men and women as sexual creatures. Point out, in fairness, that some homosexuals develop this type of sexual preference without being directly responsible for the cause. Make a distinction between a homosexual who, in spite of the strong urgings he feels toward those of his own sex, does not engage in homosexual behavior and the one who actively leads this kind of life.

For most of you, thank God, homosexuality will not become a problem in your family. But you owe it to yourselves and your children to keep informed. This knowledge will make you more alert for possible indications of homosexual tendencies and behavior among your children's acquaintances or friends. You will also be better able to "vaccinate" your daughters against possible overtures by homosexuals.

Perhaps you are a distressed and bewildered parent of a child who is a homosexual or who has a troubled feeling of differentness when it comes to his or her sexual orientation. You may want to encourage your child to contact Quest Learning Center, Route 1, Box 224, Reading, Pennsylvania 19607. This organization is dedicated to helping those with homosexual tendencies, particularly Seventh-day Adventists. It has received the support of the General Conference because its philosophy and approach harmonize with the position the denomination took at the 1981 Spring Council.

The report in the May 21, 1981, issue of the *Adventist Review* stated: "the church must extend compassion and understanding to homosexuals seeking Christ's deliverance, restoration, and redemptive grace. It must show concern by making every effort to develop a ministry that will meet their particular needs. It is not possible for the church to condone practicing homosexuality, nor is it possible to grant 'equal rights' to such individuals within the church. The efforts of the church must be focused on individuals rather than on groups, who desire help and deliverance. The church finds it impossible to endorse organizations or individuals (1) who contend that homosexuality be considered an acceptable alternative, (2) who are satisfied with being homosexuals, and (3) who resist or reject change. The church cannot negotiate with organized groups who refer to themselves as SDA gays or lesbians, nor can it establish 'diplomatic relations' with such groups when doing so might be considered recognition and official endorsement of a deviant philosophy and life style."

The latter chapters of this book deal with disturbing subjects, but because of the world you and your children live in, parents cannot dismiss these issues from consideration. (I have a chapter on venereal diseases in the book for teens.) Please recall, however, that my fundamental aim is to assist you in your primary role as sex educators for your children.

May I add a few more thoughts as I say goodbye (God be with you)?

As Adventists, we believe that prophecy teaches us that the end is quite near, and we recognize that conditions will worsen rapidly and radically as that time approaches. Therefore, we need to protect our children on every vulnerable point. At the same time, never forget that Jesus loves your children more than you do and has made all the resources of His grace available to Christian parents.

I particularly draw comfort from this statement in *The Desire of Ages*: "Whatever your anxieties and trials, spread out your case before the Lord. Your spirit will be braced for endurance. The way will be opened for you to disentangle yourself from embarrassment and difficulty."—page 329. That word *embarrassment* touches me deeply. Jesus not only forgives and helps, but He tries to spare us from the emotionally painful consequences of actions and words that can produce embarrassment.

Most of the parents of the children in my classes have not shared all our religious convictions. They, too, have shared a deep concern to properly educate their children in sexual matters. And they wanted this instruction to be based on the belief that God our Creator endowed us with the gift of sex.

Many times you will intuitively do what is best (especially you mothers). Remember, though, that some of the finest parents in the church have never had one hour of formal classwork on marriage and the family or child psychology. So don't sell yourself short or become overawed by the Niagara of advice (including this book) pouring down upon you.

The more your children perceive you as loving authority figures who reflect the heavenly Father, the more you can expect His aid in reaching and shaping your children's hearts and minds.

May God bless you as you continue filling the most important role of all—parenthood.

Bibliography

(To distinguish books that are basically religious from those that are not, the initials R and S are used, for *religious* and *secular*.)

Amstutz, H. C., M.D. *Growing Up to Love.* Scottsdale, Pennsylvania: Herald Press (Mennonite), 1956. R

Bausch, W. J. *A Boy's Sex Life.* Notre Dame, Indiana: Fides Publishers, Inc. (Roman Catholic), 1971. R

Block, William A., M.D. *What Your Child Really Wants to Know About Sex and Why.* Greenwich, Connecticut: Fawcett Crest, 1972. S

Crider, C. C., and E. C. Kistler. *The Seventh-day Adventist Family.* Berrien Springs, Michigan: Andrews University Press, 1979. R

Diagram Group. *Man's Body* (an Owner's Manual). New York: Bantam Books, 1977. S

Woman's Body, 1977. U.S.A.: Grosset and Dunlap; United Kingdom: Paddington Press Ltd; Canada: Random House of Canada Ltd.; Australia: Angus and Robertson Propriety Ltd. S

Drakeford, John W. *A Christian View of Homosexuality.* Nashville, Tennessee: Broadman Press, 1977. R

Duvall, Evelyn M. *Why Wait Till Marriage?* New York: Association Press, 1965. S

Fitch, William. *Christian Perspectives on Sex and Marriage.* Grand Rapids, Michigan: Wm. B. Erdmans Pub. Co., 1971. R

Ginott, H. G. *Between Parent and Child.* New York: Macmillan, 1965. S

Glassberg, B. Y., M.D. *Teen-age Sex Counselor.* Woodbury, New York: Barron's Educational Series, Inc., 1965. S

Gordon, Sol. *You Would If You Loved Me.* New York: Bantam Books, 1978. S

Grant, W. W., M.D. *From Parent to Child About Sex.* Grand Rapids, Michigan: Zondervan Pub. House, 1973. S

Guttmacher, A. F., M.D. *Understanding Sex.* New York: New American Library, Inc., 1970. S

Hulme, William, *Youth Considers Sex.* New York: Nelson and Sons, 1965. R

Janus, Sam. *The Death of Innocence.* New York: William Morrow and Co., 1981. S

Johnson, E. W., and Corinne Johnson. *Love and Sex and Growing Up.* New York: J. B. Lippincott, 1970. S

Jones, H. K. *Toward a Christian Understanding of the Homosexual.* New York: Association Press, 1966. R

Kelly, G. F. *Learning About Sex.* Woodbury, New York: Barrons Educational Series, Inc., 1976. S

Klingbell, Reinhard. *VD Is Not for Me.* Nashville: Southern Publishing Association (Seventh-day Adventist), 1976. R

Knight, John F., M.B., B.S. (Syd.) (Standard Medical degree issued by universities to doctors in British countries.)

What a Young Man Ought to Know About Sex. Mountain View, California: Pacific Press Publishing Association, 1977. R

What a Young Woman Ought to Know About Sex. Mountain View, California: Pacific Press Publishing Association (Seventh-day Adventist), 1977. R

Kortrey, W. *Update on Love, Sex and Life.* (Based on materials prepared by Marjory Bracker). Philadelphia: Lutheran Church Press, 1974. R

———, Teacher's Guide to the above. R

Landers, Ann. *Ann Landers Speaks Out.* Greenwich, Connecticut: Fawcett Publications, Inc. 1972-1975. S

Learning Technology Incorporated. *How to Talk With Children About Sex.* New York: John Wiley, and Sons, Inc. 1973. S

Meier, Paul D., M.D. *Christian Child-rearing and Personality Development.* Grand Rapids, Michigan: Baker Book House, 1977. R

Miles, H. J. *Sexual Understanding Before Marriage.* Grand Rapids, Michigan: Zondervan Publishing House, 1971. R

Pomeroy, W. B. *Boys and Sex.* New York: Delacorte Press, 1968. S

———, *Girls and Sex.* New York: Dell Publishing Co., 1969. S

Preston, H. *How to Teach Your Children About Sex.* Chatsworth: California: Books for Better Living, 1974. S

Ratcliff, J. D. *Your Body and How It Works.* Reader's Digest and Delacorte Press, 1975. S

Rubin, I., and L. A. Kirkendall. *Sex in the Childhood Years.* New York: Association Press, 1970. S

Sarrel, Lorna J., and P. M. Sarrel, M.D. *Sexual Unfolding*. Boston: Little, Brown and Co., 1979. S

Scanzoni, Letha. *Sex Is a Parent Affair*. Glendale, California: G/L Publications, 1973. S

Schiller, Patricia. *Creative Approach to Sex Education and Counseling*. New York: Association Press, 1973. S

Short, R. E. *Sex, Love, or Infatuation*. Minneapolis, Minnesota: Augsburg Publishing House, 1978. R

Storaska, F. *How to Say No to a Rapist and Survive*. New York: Random House, 1975. S

White, E. G. *A Solemn Appeal*. Battle Creek, Michigan: Steam Press of the Seventh-day Adventist Publishing Association, 1870. R

White, James, editor. *A Solemn Appeal Relative to Solitary Vice and the Abuses and Excesses of the Marriage Relation*. Battle Creek, Michigan: Seventh-day Adventist Publishing Association (a verbatim reset edition of the original 1870 edition). R

Wyden, Peter and Barbara. *Growing Up Straight* (What Every Thoughtful Parent Should Know About Homosexuality). New York: Stein and Day, 1968. S

Lutheran Church—Missouri Synod Series.

- Frey, Marguerite K. *I Wonder, I Wonder*. Kindergarten through grade 3. 1967. R
- Hummel, Ruth S. *Wonderfully Made*. Grades 4 through 6. 1967. R
- Bueltmann. *Take the High Road*. Junior high. 1967. R
- Witt, E. N. *Life Can Be Sexual*. High school. 1967. R
- Kolb, E. J. *Parents' Guide to Christian Conversation About Sex*. 1967. R
- Wessler, M. F. *Christian View of Sex Education. A Manual for Church Leaders*. St. Louis, Missouri: Concordia Publishing House, 1967. R

United Methodist Church

- Johnson, E. B. *Youth Views Sexuality*, 1971. R
- Blanchard, Anne C. Course Design Guide for above. R
- ———, *Sexually Speaking—Who Am I?* 1973. R
- Patterson, W. G. Course Design Guide for above. Nashville, Tennessee: The Methodist Publishing House. R